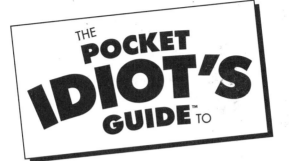

THE
POCKET
IDIOT'S
GUIDE TO

Hinduism

by Cybelle Shattuck,
adapted by Nancy D. Lewis

ALPHA
A Pearson Education Company

Adapted from the original, published as *Religions of the World: Hinduism, First Edition,* by Cybelle Shattuck, published by Pearson Education, Inc., publishing as Prentice Hall, Copyright © 1999 Lawrence King Publishing Ltd.

***The Pocket Idiot's Guide to Hinduism* published by Pearson Education, Inc., publishing as Alpha Books, Copyright © 2003, Laurence King Publishing Ltd.**

International Standard Book Number: 0-02864482-4
Library of Congress Catalog Card Number: 2002115291

04 03 02   8 7 6 5 4 3 2 1

Interpretation of the printing code: The rightmost number of the first series of numbers is the year of the book's printing; the rightmost number of the second series of numbers is the number of the book's printing. For example, a printing code of 02-1 shows that the first printing occurred in 2002.

Printed in the United States of America

For marketing and publicity, please call: 317-581-3722

The publisher offers discounts on this book when ordered in quantity for bulk purchases and special sales.

For sales within the United States, please contact: Corporate and Government Sales, 1-800-382-3419 or corpsales@pearsontechgroup.com

Outside the United States, please contact: International Sales, 317-581-3793 or international@pearsontechgroup.com

Contents

Introduction

Hindu terms are becoming more and more a part of everyday vocabulary. Most Americans are familiar with words like reincarnation, guru, and mantra. And yet, in spite of the adoption of these terms and a general understanding of their meaning, few Westerners have any real awareness of how these borrowed ideas fit into the larger framework of Hinduism.

By focusing on texts and philosophies, we have taken ideas out of context. This book tries to provide the missing context by presenting the historical development of philosophical ideas only as a starting point for examining the way Hindus live out their traditions. Emphasis is placed particularly on modern practices and the factors that are currently shaping religious life.

Extras

The sidebars in this book offer extra information and help to explain the topics and terms throughout the book. Use these as road signs on the journey to understanding Hinduism.

On the Right Path

These boxes provide guidance about Hinduism, which supplement the materials in the text. They take a topic one step further toward understanding the religion.

Hindu Hints

These boxes will be filled with tips about the text to supplement information on the topic at hand.

Brahma Says

Brahma is known to Hindus as the creator of the Universe, so if Brahma speaks we should listen! These boxes define vocabulary terms and jargon familiar to Hinduism that are used in the text. Understanding the typical vocabulary and jargon of the religion helps you better understand the general subject when you encounter these terms in another context.

Bet You Didn't Know

These boxes are extra tidbits of background information that are informative or just plain interesting.

Trademarks

All terms mentioned in this book that are known to be or are suspected of being trademarks or service marks have been appropriately capitalized. Alpha Books and Pearson Education, Inc., cannot attest to the accuracy of this information. Use of a term in this book should not be regarded as affecting the validity of any trademark or service mark.

Chapter 1

Introduction to Hinduism and Hindus

In This Chapter

- What Hinduism and Hindu really mean
- The concept of "religion"
- The languages of India
- The diverse Indian culture

Hinduism has become a global tradition. In South Asia, it is the dominant religion of India and Nepal, it is a minority tradition in Sri Lanka, and it has small memberships in Pakistan and Bangladesh. In Southeast Asia, a few Hindu enclaves, most notably on the Indonesian island of Bali, stand as remnants of large populations who arrived in the medieval period. There are also new growing Hindu populations in urban centers like Singapore and Kuala Lumpur.

Outside of Asia, well-established Hindu communities exist in eastern and southern Africa, in the

Persian Gulf states, on the islands of Fiji, on the northeast coast of South America, in the Caribbean, in North America, and in Europe. In spite of this globalization, Hinduism is still irrevocably linked to the culture of South Asia and any understanding of the Hindu tradition must begin with the land of India.

Distinguishing Hinduism from Hindus

The term Hinduism is of recent origin, having been applied mostly by Westerners to denote the majority religion of India. Only groups that had clear non-Hindu identities, such as Jains, Buddhists, Parsis, Muslims, Jews, and Christians, were not included in the generic Hindu category. The use of a foreign designation derives from the fact that there is no corresponding word indigenous to South Asia.

The people of South Asia generally define themselves according to local caste and community, and among these, there is no single scripture, deity, or religious teacher common to all that can be designated as the core of Hinduism. Yet the very vagueness of the term makes it useful. This is because the word Hinduism comes from Hindu, a name used by medieval Muslims to refer to the people living around the Sindu (Indus) River. The term Hindu then became an umbrella term for all the people residing in the Indian subcontinent. Hence, Hinduism, as the religious faith indigenous to the Indians, includes most of the regional traditions that developed in India.

Indian religions that define themselves as non-Hindu, like Buddhism and Jainism, had to develop clear boundaries to distinguish themselves from the Hindus. But Hinduism itself has never evolved such clear boundaries—religious practices across the subcontinent show great regional variation. The vague quality of the term Hinduism makes it a convenient designation for the varied traditions of approximately 80 percent of the people in India and their kindred communities around the world. It is important, however, to remember that the word is a modern invention and that to project "Hindu" religion back through time is to use an artificial category in order to distinguish the roots of modern Hinduism from other Indian religions.

"Religion" = Dharma

Just as there is no indigenous word to designate the religion of India, so, too, there is no one word equivalent to the Western concept of "religion." Perhaps the word that comes closest is *dharma*, which means law, duty, justice, and virtuousness. Like Western "morality," it refers to both religious and social obligations of behavior. As such, the term brings out the emphasis on *praxis*, or correct behavior, that is central to the Hindu worldview.

To understand what constitutes dharmic behavior, you must understand the Hindu worldview. Foundational to this worldview is the belief that the sacred is immanent in the world. The natural world, social order, and family life all have correlations to divine order. Because of this, all actions, whether ostensibly secular or obviously religious, have religious implications. This means that your place within the world order affects your *dharma*. The immanence of the sacred also gives religious significance to things that may not seem religious in Western traditions, such as places, objects, people, and moments in time.

On the Right Path

Hinduism is a religion that focuses on behavior more than belief. There is great diversity in beliefs, there are different deities, philosophies, and paths, but all of these require adherence to particular rules of behavior.

Speaking of Hinduism

The body of religious beliefs and practices covered by the overarching term of Hinduism is one of the most richly diverse religions in history. This is a natural condition for a tradition that developed organically, over thousands of years, out of the interactions of the various peoples who have settled in South Asia. The wealth of human diversity is also evident in the languages of the subcontinent.

There are four distinct language families, Indo-European, Dravidian, Tibeto-Burman, and

Austro-Asiatic. From these come the 17 official languages recognized in India, each with its countless dialects, and the minor, unofficial languages spoken in modern South Asia. Indo-European languages descended from Sanskrit are spoken in northern India and Nepal, and include languages like Hindi, Marathi, Bengali, and Nepali. Four Dravidian languages, Tamil, Telegu, Malayalam, and Kannada, are spoken in the four states of south India. The other two language families have much smaller numbers of speakers. Tibeto-Burman languages are used in the Himalayan and northeastern areas such as the Katmandu valley. Austro-Asiatic languages are still spoken by tribal peoples who can be found in central, eastern, and northeastern India.

Most of these languages are associated with specific regions. This regionalism, one of the hallmarks of Hinduism, is a byproduct of South Asian geography.

Cultural Diversity

The subcontinent of India has geographically defined regions that have developed their own distinctive cultures. The northern boundary is formed by the Himalayan mountain range. These mountains have not prevented immigration, especially from the northwest. Peoples entering from that direction settled in the river valleys of the north, where they interacted with the previous inhabitants.

As these immigrants gradually worked their way across to the eastern areas their cultures were continually modified. So, for example, the descendants of an Indo-European tribe that had come into India from the northwest would have a considerably altered culture by the time they reached the eastern coast. Thus, the northwest and the northeast developed distinct cultures, even when the influences that came together in each region had similar origins.

Within the subcontinent, the distinctive geographical cultures have also been shaped by the necessity of adapting to their climates. In the northern plains, populations have clustered around the rivers that provide resources for agriculture. One such region centers on the rivers of the Punjab in the northwest, and a second exists along the Ganges and Yamuna Rivers in the northern plains. Most of the great urban centers of modern India in these areas are also the sacred centers of Hindu history.

Separate regional cultures exist in the Himalayan Mountains, where life must be adapted to a rugged environment, and on the coasts, where fishing adds an alternate source of sustenance to the diet. The subcontinent is divided north from south by the Vindhya Mountains. Within the south, where the Dravidian language family is dominant, there are distinct regional cultures in the Deccan Plateau and among the mountains along both sea coasts. The southern climate is suited to different agricultural products and forms of animal husbandry than the plains of the north. Finally, a further cultural diversity is found among the small "tribal" groups, many of which live in fringe areas, especially in the mountains.

Bet You Didn't Know

Within each cultural region, there are also pluralities caused by society. Three quarters of India is still rural, living in villages and focused on agriculture. But the urban areas are growing and having a tremendous impact on traditions. There is now a middle class nearly equal in size to the population of the whole United States. This middle class, urban and educated, is changing the character of Hinduism. Furthermore, they are having a disproportionate impact on global Hinduism because the majority of the emigrants living in other parts of the world come from this urban class.

Each of the South Asian regional cultures has its own languages, foods, art, music, architecture, deities, and rituals. Social hierarchies and marital systems vary from area to area. Within a region, local communities have their own deities, myths, and traditions. The gods and festivals of one village may not be recognized in another area. This is why it is so difficult to define Hinduism except to say that it is, as the word implies, the religion that developed in India and is practiced by the majority of Indians and Nepalis.

And yet, despite the diversity, there is a general Hindu worldview. The names of the deities and the explanations of the rituals may vary but a person from the Punjab (in the northwest) can watch a person from Tamil Nadu (in the southeast) celebrate an unfamiliar festival to an unknown deity and have a sense of kinship.

In the next chapters, you will begin to understand some of the beliefs and practices shared by the diverse traditions that sit within the shade of the Hindu "umbrella."

The Least You Need to Know

- The term Hinduism is of recent origin, having been applied mostly by Westerners to denote the majority religion of India.

- There is no one word equivalent to the Western concept of "religion"; the word that comes closest is dharma—meaning law, duty, justice, and virtuousness—which refers to both religious and social obligations of behavior.

- There are four distinct language families, Indo-European, Dravidian, Tibeto-Burman, and Austro-Asiatic. From these come the 17 official languages recognized in India, each with its countless dialects, and the minor, unofficial languages spoken in modern South Asia.

- The subcontinent of India has geographically defined regions that have developed their own distinctive cultures. Within the subcontinent, the distinctive geographical cultures have also been shaped by the necessity of adapting to their climates.

Chapter 2

The Indus Valley and the Vedas

In This Chapter

- The culture of the Indus Valley
- Understanding the Vedic materials
- The celestial, atmospheric, and earthly realms
- In the beginning ...

The roots of Hindu tradition can be traced back to the earliest civilizations in India. Over time, the beliefs and practices of the various peoples who migrated into the subcontinent and took up residence have interacted so that the modern tradition is an amalgamation of influences brought together through thousands of years. The two foundational influences of which we have information (and hence this chapter) were the cultures of the Indus Valley civilization and the Indo-Europeans. Each of these contributed to the development of the religious traditions that became Hinduism.

Indus Valley Civilization

The earliest civilization in India is known as the Indus Valley civilization because archeologists have excavated major cities in the Indus River Valley. The two largest cities excavated are known as Mohenjo Daro and Harappa.

The Indus culture developed from about 2500 B.C.E. (although its origins go all the way back to the Neolithic Period, 7000–6000 B.C.E.) and reached its peak around 2300–2000 B.C.E. During that period it had trade links with Mesopotamia. The Indus culture was, at its height, quite extensive. Archeological evidence from the mature Indus civilization has been found at more than 1,500 sites covering an area from the upper Ganga-Yamuna river valley in the east to the Iranian border in the west and down to the Gujarat coast. The Indus culture began to decline by 1900 B.C.E. and had faded away by 1500 B.C.E.

The cities of the Indus Valley were remarkably well organized. Mohenjo Daro and Harappa each housed about 40,000 people. The cities were laid out in organized grid patterns, and residence areas appear to have been determined by occupation.

Bet You Didn't Know

Sophisticated water technologies in the Indus Valley provided drainage systems and wells for most houses, and large tanks may have served as central bathing areas.

Large storehouses in the Indus towns suggest that the economy was grain-based, like ancient Mesopotamia. The people of the Indus Valley had a written script, examples of which are found on small clay seals, but this script has not been deciphered, so most of the theories about this early civilization are based on deductions drawn from archeological evidence.

There are several artifacts that suggest religious practices similar to those found in later South Asian traditions. First, there are numerous terra cotta figurines of a female with wide hips, prominent breasts, and an elaborate headdress. Scholars speculate that this image may be a goddess associated with human and agricultural fertility. Second, there are images of animals, some natural and others mythical, on small clay seals. One seal depicts a human figure standing in pipal trees with a row of what seem to be worshipers below. These may be precursors to the reverence for certain trees and animals found in later ages. There are also a few seals that show a figure seated in what may be a *yoga* posture. Finally, the great water tanks may indicate an early concern with bathing and ritual purity.

Brahma Says

Yoga, from the Sanskrit root yuj "to yoke, unite, control," refers to disciplines of asceticism and meditation that lead to knowledge inaccessible to ordinary human consciousness. Yoga is used in both Hinduism and Buddhism.

The Early Vedic Age

Between 2000 and 1500 B.C.E., people from Central Asia began a great migration. Some settled in areas across western and northern Europe, others went south and east into Iran and then India. The latter groups called themselves *Aryans*, a term that in India later came to designate particular social classes. Because of the ancient connections between these far-flung immigrants, the peoples of India, Iran, and Europe all belong to the Indo-European language family. *Sanskrit*, Persian, Latin, and their modern descendants are all related.

Brahma Says

In reference to the people who invaded the Indic lands, the **Aryans** were an ethnic group who spoke a particular language (Sanskrit). You might also be familiar with the term "Aryan" in regards to the (distantly related, but not the same) light-skinned, light-hair, and light-eyed people popularized in Germany and by other fascists as a "supreme race" in the twentieth century. **Sanskrit** is to the north Indian languages what Latin is to the Romance languages—both are also dead. The relationship between Sanskrit and other European languages is close and can be seen in the comparison of key words. For instance, English "brother" is "phrater" in Greek and "bhratar" in Sanskrit.

The Indo-European immigrants entered India in the northwest and then moved into the area around the Ganges River, which was also inhabited by the descendants of the Indus Valley civilization. The Aryans became the dominant force in northern India and gradually their influence spread to the south. Over time the indigenous agricultural social systems were blended with the migrants' culture to form the amalgamation that produced classical Indian civilization.

The Indo-Europeans were a nomadic, rural people, and their religious traditions were portable. When they settled in India, they brought with them the sacred language of Sanskrit, belief in a pantheon of deities, religious practices centered around a fire sacrifice, and a hierarchical social structure.

The Vedas

The earliest religious compositions in India are the Indo-European Sanskrit texts, the Vedas. The word *veda* means knowledge, and these texts contained information necessary to the performance of sacred fire rituals. It is difficult to date the texts accurately, but scholars believe they were composed between 1500 and 600 B.C.E. These Vedas were preserved orally. Priestly families passed on the texts from generation to generation, using elaborate mnemonic systems to preserve them accurately.

Brahma Says _____

Veda is a Sanskrit word that means "knowledge" or "wisdom."

Ritual Materials

In the most limited sense, the Vedas are "collections" (*samhitas*) of ritual material:

- The *Rig Veda Samhita* contains 10 books of hymns to various deities. Each of these books was composed by sages belonging to the priestly families who were responsible for preserving the hymnal lore. Priests recited these hymns during the fire rituals.

- The *Sama Veda Samhita* is a book of songs based on the *Rig Veda* with instructions for their recitation.

- The *Yajur Veda* contains short prose formulae and verses, or mantras (a sacred word or formula used in some forms of ritual as a hymn or meditation), used in ritual.

- The *Atharva Veda* is a collection of hymns and magical formulae, many of which are not related to the sacrificial ritual, but to matters of daily life.

> **Hindu Hints**
>
> The *Atharva Veda* was the latest addition and has not been given the same status as the first three Vedic Samhitas, a circumstance that has led scholars to suggest that it may reflect popular, non-Aryan traditions rather than those of the priesthood. Many of the formulae in the *Atharva Veda* are for ordinary concerns like curing diseases, warding off harmful spirits, and the prevention of snakebite.

Additional Materials

Each of the Vedic "collections" has three types of additional material and the wider use of the word Veda includes all of these:

- The first additions, which concern ritual exegesis, are called *Brahmanas*. The Brahmanas describe rules for the rituals and give explanations about their purposes and meanings.

- The second additions are called "compositions of the forest" (*Aranyakas*), because, according to tradition, they were composed in the forest by solitary sages. The Aranyakas mostly supplement the Brahmanas, focusing on rites that were not developed in detail in the earlier texts. They also elaborate on the importance of knowing the meaning of rituals by describing the extra benefits that accrue to the ritual performer through this special information.

- The third type of additional material, the *Upanishads*, further developed the ideas of the Aranyakas by explaining the true nature and meaning of the rituals in an age when the focus was shifting away from performance and toward knowledge. The Upanishads are the latest additions, and were probably composed between 600 and 300 B.C.E.

Although the Vedas are revered as sacred texts, very few modern Hindus know much about them. A few hymns are recited regularly in temple and household liturgies, but the texts are primarily ritual manuals, and the bulk of their contents is only studied by priests and scholars. In spite of this, they have tremendous authority in Hindu tradition.

The Vedas are described as *shruti*, "that which was heard" by the ancient sages. The texts contain knowledge that is considered transhuman and eternal. This knowledge was revealed to the sages when they were in meditative states. Some theistic schools believe God authored the Vedas, but others believe the texts are authorless. They simply exist as eternal knowledge, and the Vedic *rishis* ("seers") were able to "see" that knowledge and transmit it to others.

Gods of the Cosmos

The gods hymned in the Vedas form a pantheon associated with natural and cultural forces. So, for example, there are deities identified with the sun, moon, earth, sky, wind, and night. There are also gods and goddesses with specific cultural spheres like warfare, healing, and ritual. The divinities, called *devas*, can be loosely organized according to their place within the three levels of the cosmos: the celestial realm, the atmospheric realm, and the earthly realm.

 Brahma Says

> A **deva** is a deity. For example, Vishnu, Shiva, and Devi are Hindu gods or "deities." See Chapter 5 for more information.

The Celestial Realm

Of particular importance in the celestial realm is the god Varuna, the lord of order (*rita*, which means the cosmic order). Order is the opposite of chaos, and Varuna is petitioned to maintain righteousness and prevent the cosmos from dissolving in chaos. This tension between order and chaos is a theme in the Vedas and in subsequent Indian religions. Varuna is often accompanied by Mitra, the

god of night, who is also lord of social contracts.
Together they represent cosmic and social order.

The Atmospheric Realm

Among the atmospheric gods, the most notable is
Indra, the warrior deity associated with the thunder-
storm. Especially in the earlier Vedic hymns, Indra is
the leader of the gods as is appropriate for a warrior
culture. Indra is credited with conquering the lands
in which the Aryans live and subduing their enemies.
His most famous myth involves the destruction of
a snake, symbolizing chaos, and the release of the
waters of the sky. As the Aryans become settled,
the warrior god loses prominence.

Bet You Didn't Know

One of the striking aspects of the
Vedic hymns is the tendency to address all
the deities in similar terms. Thus a hymn
to Agni may state that Agni is supreme,
although another hymn will say the same
thing of Indra. Some hymns even identify
one god with another, making statements
such as "You, O Agni, are Indra." These
passages seem to be intended as statements of praise, but they also make the
specific roles and identities of the deities
fluid, and allow gods who gain popularity
to supplant older deities with relative ease.
Thus the membership and hierarchy of the
Vedic pantheon shifts continuously.

The Earthly Realm

In the earthly realm, the most important deities are Agni, the fire god; Soma, god of the drink consumed during the fire sacrifice (see the section that follows); and Brihaspati, the patron of the priests. All of these deities are directly connected to the fire sacrifice. They act as mediators between humans and the gods of the upper regions. Brihaspati is the arbiter of the ritual and Soma is a necessary participant. But Agni, who is both god of fire and the fire itself, is the medium in which the sacrifice takes place. It is Agni who carries the offerings up to the heavens in his smoke. He also carries the dead to the realm of Yama, the lord of death.

Fire Sacrifice

The fire sacrifice was the means of communion between humanity and the gods. The ritual may have begun as a simple hospitality rite, in which deities were invited to a celebration. Offerings were placed in the fire to be conveyed to the gods by Agni, the lord of fire. Over time the ritual grew more elaborate and gained greater significance until it became so important that it was thought an error in its performance might jeopardize the order of the cosmos, and throw the universe into chaos.

There were two types of fire sacrifice:

- *grihya* ("domestic") rites for the household
- *shrauta* ("based on *shruti*"—i.e. the Vedas) were the public rites

The domestic rites required only one fire and could be performed by the householders themselves. The object of these rites was to gain material rewards on earth such as health, long life, the birth of sons, and wealth in the form of cattle. Simple offerings of cooked food were made daily at the household fire to Agni and the creator god Prajapati in the morning and to Surya (sun god) and Prajapati in the evening. Household rituals also celebrated the new moon and full moon, the seasons of the year, the first fruits of harvest, and special family events such as the building of a new house, the birth of a son, and the important stages of a child's life. Even when rituals like marriage rites were performed by a priest, the family had major roles in the ceremonies, which were held at the domestic fire.

The *shrauta* rites were, naturally, more elaborate. Instead of using the domestic fire, they required three special fires and several priests, each with his own specific duty. First the fire altars had to be constructed. There was no permanent sacred site for these rituals, undoubtedly a reflection of the earlier nomadic lifestyle of the Indo-European migrants. Altars were oriented to the compass points and built in specific shapes, circular, semicircular, and square. The altars were usually raised mounds made of sand, earth, pebbles, and pieces of wood. The shapes identified the fires. The round altar represented the earth, the square was the four-directional sky, and the semicircle was the atmosphere between earth and the heavens.

As the rituals became more elaborate, several priests were employed. One priest was responsible for reciting hymns from the *Rig Veda*, another sang songs from the *Sama Veda*, a third performed the manual jobs of making offerings and pouring oblations, while a fourth oversaw the entire proceeding to ensure that no mistakes were made.

Bet You Didn't Know

The *shrauta* rites included sacrifices that devoted to Agni and Soma, for whom offering of milk, clarified butter, vegetable cakes, animals, or stalks of the soma plant would be placed into the fire.

Sacrifice and Creation

As the sacrificial ritual gained greater and greater importance, the gods associated with that ritual eclipsed the deities of the older Vedic hymns. This is particularly evident in the case of Agni. In one hymn Agni is addressed as Indra, Vishnu, Brahman-aspati, Varuna, Mitra, etc., and is said to be all the gods. As the messenger of the gods, who links humanity with the deities, Agni personified the power of the sacrifice.

Another deity elevated by association with the sacrifice was Vach, speech personified as a goddess. In

the Brahmanas, she is connected to creation and ritual. One story describes how the devas were able to
institute rituals that sustain the world and produce
bounty, life, and immortality for the gods only with
her help. Without speech, there would be no ritual
hymns or mantras, and thus no ritual power.

I've Got the Power

The power of the sacrifice was embodied in the sounds
of the sacrifice, the Vedic hymns that were uttered by
the priests. That power was called *brahman*, and the
priests who wielded it were the *brahmanas* or Brahmins
("having to do with Brahman"). This term referred
to their knowledge and use of the power of Brahman
contained in ritual sounds and speech. Gradually the
ritual speech, deified as the goddess Vach, came to be
seen as the basis of the entire cosmos.

Hindu Hints

Hopefully this will help clarify some
things: Brahma is the creator god, and
brahman is divine power, the power of the
Vedic mantras. Brahman (capitalized) is
also the Absolute. *Brahmana* is a text that
explains the performance and meaning of
the Vedic rituals. Brahmin is the priestly
caste (*varna*).

The power of the ritual sound is so great that the
gods themselves were thought to have performed

sacrifices in order to reach their place in heaven. The gods, like the seers, know the true basis of things, the power of Brahman. But this also means that the gods are no longer supreme, they have no ultimate power. They are part of the manifested cosmos, not the primordial creators. This change in the status and role of the gods was part of a change in the conception of the cosmos.

The power of speech accounted for the forms of the manifest cosmos, but not the origin. It was no longer possible to credit any of the gods with the role of creator, since they were now seen as part of the creation, so later hymns puzzled over the problem of the creative process. One famous text, *Rig Veda* X.129, directly addresses the problem of where creation comes from. Noting that the gods cannot know the truth, because they only came after the creation of the world, the hymn asks the question, "Who then knows whence [this creation] has arisen?" The final verse says that only the one who looks down from the highest heaven can know—and maybe even he does not know.

How It All Began

Although the sages were not certain who/what set the creation in motion, they knew how it was done. Some hymns ascribed creation to either a divine craftsman (RV X.81), or a smith (RV X.72), or a cosmic embryo (RV X.121), but in all these, the model of the process of creation was the fire sacrifice. The ritual of the sacrifice was the basis for the entire cosmos because the cosmos came from the sacrifice. This idea was made explicit in the famous *Purusha Sukta* (RV X.90), the "Hymn to the Person." The hymn has two basic parts. The first part describes the cosmic person, or Purusha, and establishes an identity between the Purusha and the universe.

> The Purusha has a thousand heads, a thousand eyes, and a thousand feet. He pervaded the world on all sides and extended beyond it as far as ten fingers. The Purusha alone is all this universe, what has been, and what will be. He rules likewise over [the world of] immortality [viz., the gods], which he grows beyond through food. Such is the extent of his greatness; and the Purusha is still greater than this. A quarter of him is all beings, three quarters are [the world of] the immortal in heaven. (RV X.90.1–3)

In this passage, the Purusha is the entire universe. One quarter of the Person makes up the manifest world of created beings, the other three quarters form the immortal, upper regions.

The second part of the hymn describes the sacrifice of Purusha and gives a lengthy account of correlations between the sacrificed body and the features of the universe. In this way, the sacrifice is both the agency and the substance of the cosmos. The moon comes from his mind, the sun from his eye, the wind god from his breath, from his navel comes the atmosphere, from his feet comes the earth, and from his ear the directions. The correlations between the

Purusha and the cosmos also extend to human society. The Brahmin priests are said to have come from Purusha's mouth and the ruling class (*rajanya*, later called *Kshatriya*) from his arms. From his thighs came the *Vaishyas*, a word that literally means "people" and refers to artisans, merchants, and farmers. And from the feet came the *Shudras*, the servant class.

This hymn contains the first listing of the four social classes that later became a basis for social and religious precepts. The specific associations may seem arbitrary, but the idea that the cosmos, the world of nature, human society, and the sacrifice are parallel orders of reality is foundational to later religious traditions in India.

The Least You Need to Know

- The Indus culture developed from about 2500 B.C.E. (although its origins go all the way back to the Neolithic Period, 7000–6000 B.C.E.) and reached its peak around 2300–2000 B.C.E.

- The Indo-Europeans were a nomadic, rural people, and their religious traditions were portable. When they settled in India, they brought with them the sacred language of Sanskrit, belief in a pantheon of deities, religious practices centered around a fire sacrifice, and a hierarchical social structure.

- The *Rig Veda Samhita* contains 10 books of hymns to various deities; *Sama Veda Samhita* is a book of songs; *Yajur Veda* contains short prose formulae and verses; *Atharva Veda* is a collection of hymns and magical formulae.

Chapter **3**

Speculation in the Upanishads

In This Chapter

- Thought replaces physical actions
- Underlying fabric of the universe
- Escaping the cycle of rebirth
- Control of the senses
- What to do, and not to do

Gradually the sacred knowledge associated with the sacrifice became internalized. The ritual was extended to include mental performance, in which thought replaced physical actions. Sages taught that knowledge was primary, not the external ritual.

This chapter will cover some of the topics that were taught, as well as who had to follow the teachings.

Intense Philosophical Speculation

The Aranyakas, the forest books, reflect the teachings of sages who lived in forest retreats, and allegorized the sacrificial tradition. This internalization of ritual placed new emphasis on the individual person, who was the medium of the mental ritual. He became like the Brahmin priest, meditating on the meaning of the sacrifice and attaining the sacred knowledge. This process of reinterpreting religious practices and knowledge was continued in the Upanishads.

The Upanishads reflect an era of intense philosophical speculation, the same era that produced Buddhism and Jainism. This speculation was carried out in schools where teachers passed on their ideas to their students and took part in large public discussions. The public meetings were gatherings where great sages, both men and women, could share ideas and debate their merits. Most of the Upanishadic material is in the form of scholarly debates and teacher-student dialogues.

Brahman and Atman: The Nature of the Cosmos

One of the most significant issues of the period was the nature of the cosmos. In the later Vedas, sages suggested a single Absolute underlaid all existence. Speculations about the nature of that One focused on food, speech, breath, or the creator god,

Prajapati. But, over time, the *brahman* superseded these others. As early as the *Atharva Veda*, some hymns had moved beyond defining *brahman* as the power of sacred speech and the sacrifice, and had begun to speak of it as a cosmic principle.

So, for example, *brahman* is "the womb of both the existent and the nonexistent" (1.4.1), and in another hymn, the earth, sky, and atmosphere are all established by *brahman* (10.2.25). In these passages, the old Vedic definition of *brahman* as the power of the sacred speech and the sacrifice is replaced by the understanding that *brahman* is the ultimate, underlying essence of the universe. This Absolute is designated by the universal form, *Brahman*.

In the Upanishads, *Brahman* supersedes all the Vedic *devas*. Earlier texts had already deprived the gods of their ultimate superiority by making their existence dependent on creation. The gods came into existence after creation, and only gained their power and immortality through the sacrificial ritual. The supreme place now belonged to *Brahman*, conceptualized as a Supreme Deity in some texts and an impersonal Absolute in others.

A passage in the *Brihadaranyaka Upanishad* (III.9.1,9) seems to identify the *devas* as the various powers of the *Brahman*. Here, the sage Yajnavalkya is asked how many gods there are. He says that there are 3,306 gods. Asked again how many gods there are really, he says there are 33. This process of reduction continues until he says there is only one god. Later he defines that One as *Brahman*.

The term used for *Brahman* in this passage is *sutra-atman*, "thread-Self; the Self which passes like a thread through the universe." This name for *Brahman* emphasizes its role as the underlying fabric of the universe. But *Brahman* is also called the *antary-amin*, the "Inner Controller" that exists within each being. The Upanishads devoted great energy to discussing the relationship between the external, cosmic aspect of *Brahman* and its internal aspect, usually called *atman*.

> **Brahma Says**
>
> **Atman** is defined as the individual self. The *atman* is the true Self within the individual person, the immortal, pure essence of each being.

One of the most famous passages describing the relation of *Brahman* and *atman* is a conversation between Shvetaketu and his father in the *Chandogya Upanishad* (6.12–13). Shvetaketu is instructed to break open the seed of a tree and describe what he sees. He finds nothing. His father points out that from that subtle essence of the seed that he cannot see, a great tree may grow. The whole world has this same subtle essence for its Self. The father then asks his son to dissolve salt in water and teaches him that just as the salt, which is not visible, pervades and cannot be separated from the water, so, too, the *Brahman* pervades the individual.

The *Brahman* within the individual is called the *atman*. This teaching is punctuated with the refrain *tat tvam asi*, "You are That." In this equation, You means *atman* and That means *Brahman*.

Samsara and Karman: The Cycles of Life

The concept of an individual, eternal *atman* that is identified with the universal *Brahman* changed the context and goals of religious practices. In the early Vedic hymns, the goal of the sacrifice was to procure the beneficence of the gods to ensure a good life on earth, and a safe trip to heaven after death. But in the Upanishads, the gods are no longer supreme and their heavenly abode is not a permanent, final goal.

In this era, the belief in a single life span was replaced by a system of reincarnation called *samsara*, the cycle of rebirths. According to this system, at death you would pass on to a life in heaven or hell, depending on the merits of your activities in life. Then, after a certain amount of time, the individual would be reborn on earth once again.

Brahma Says _____

Samsara is the cycle of rebirth.

The mechanism that regulated this system was *karman*, a word that literally means "action." Every action must have an effect. So, the effects of your actions in life determine what you will experience after death, and what kind of life you will have in the next birth. In this way, even if a person does not seem to receive all the rewards or punishments deserved in a particular life, the scales will be balanced in the future.

Brahma Says _____

Karman means action, the acts that affect one's experiences after death and in the next life.

The only way to stop this cycle of rebirths is to achieve *moksha*, "liberation" from *samsara*. This liberation is attained through knowledge. When you truly understand the nature of the *Brahman*, and hence the true nature of your own self (the *atman*), then there is no more accumulation of *karman* and the individual is not reborn again. The Upanishads make it clear that this liberating knowledge of *Brahman* is separate from the old wisdom of the Vedas, which is now described as "lower knowledge" that only serves to prepare you for the "higher" knowledge of *Brahman*.

Brahma Says _____

Moksha is the liberation from the cycle of rebirth through knowledge.

Control Through Yoga

Attaining the higher knowledge that brings *moksha* required great effort. The discipline known as yoga developed as a means to *moksha*. The word yoga, from the Sanskrit root *yuj* "to yoke, unite, control," refers to disciplines of asceticism and meditation that lead to knowledge inaccessible to ordinary human consciousness.

Hindu Hints

The groups of ascetics who developed these systems of discipline are called *shramanas*, "strivers" who seek liberation through austerities and meditation. They lived simple lives, casting away home and possessions in order to cultivate detachment. Out of these renouncer traditions came the monastic communities of Buddhism, Jainism, and Hinduism.

Yoga includes moral, physical, and mental discipline because the body must be controlled before it is possible to control and focus the mind to reach higher knowledge. The word yoga first appears in the *Katha Upanishad*, where it is described as control of the senses. Combined with control of mental activity, this yoga is said to lead to the supreme state. In *Katha Upanishad* (1.3.3–9), Yama, the god of death, uses the analogy of a chariot to describe the human state: the body is the chariot, the senses are the horses, and the self (*atman*) is the charioteer. Just as a charioteer controls his horses, so should a person control his senses.

The theme of controlling the body and yoking the mind to attain liberation from rebirth appears in most of the Indian religious traditions.

The classical form of Hindu yogic discipline is described in the *Yoga Sutra*, attributed to Patanjali and dated between 400 B.C.E. and 500 C.E. Patanjali defines yoga as the cessation of the fluctuations of mental activity. This is achieved by following specific steps. The first steps teach ethical, personal, and social behavior through practices such as nonviolence (*ahimsa*), truthfulness, celibacy, cleanliness, asceticism, and study. Second is a gradual development of physical control so that the external world and the body no longer distract the *yogin*. This involves sitting in specific postures, breath control, and withdrawing the senses from the outer world. Once the body and senses are under control, the yogin is able to progress through ever-deepening stages of meditation until he reaches the transcendent state of awareness that grants freedom from rebirth.

 Brahma Says

A **yogin** is one who practices yoga.

This final attainment is, essentially, the reversal of the process of creation as described in the metaphysical system of Samkhya philosophy that is associated with Patanjali's Yoga. According to Samkhya, there are two basic principles:

- Inactive Consciousness, which is called *purusha*
- Primordial Materiality, which is called *prakriti*

These two principles are completely separate from each other. Prakriti has three inherent qualities, the three *gunas:*

- *Sattva,* "purity"
- *Rajas,* "activity"
- *Tamas,* "dullness, inertia"

 Brahma Says _____

> **Gunas** are the inherent qualities of the universe. **Purusha** is the divine person. **Prakriti,** materiality, is the feminine matter from which the cosmos is formed.

When *purusha* comes too close to *prakriti,* the equilibrium of these qualities is disturbed. As a result, *prakriti* evolves the various elements that make up the manifest world. This model of the unfolding of creation is also the path for retracing the process.

The *yogin*, after training the body to allow the mind access to higher, hidden knowledge, is able to understand that the diverse forms of the human world are just manifestations of *prakriti*, and that *purusha*, the pure consciousness, is completely separate from material existence. With this knowledge of the distinction between *purusha* and *prakriti*, the *yogin* is freed from the influence of the *gunas*. Once the *gunas* cease to be effective, *purusha* and *prakriti* are once again isolated from each other.

This system of creation from the interaction of the two principles appears in other Indian traditions. The descriptions of the principles and the nature of their relationships change, but the idea of a pair playing a role in the process of creation recurs, and the description of the universe as governed by the three qualities of purity, activity, and inertia becomes part of most Indian philosophies. Later traditions elaborate and improve on the older cosmogonies in order to include different beliefs, but the idea that enlightenment involves the personal attainment of knowledge about the true nature of the self and the cosmos remains constant.

On the Right Path

Yoga, as a system of discipline through which you can retrace the process of creation and gain higher knowledge, has an important place in South Asian traditions.

Varnashrama-dharma: Defining Correct Actions

The attainment of the knowledge that leads to liberation requires intense devotion of time and energy. This is not, of course, appropriate for everybody. In fact, only a few have the impulse and the discipline to spend their lives seeking liberation. For others, what is important is to perform correct actions, which will in turn ensure benefits in the present life and an advantageous rebirth. The definition of what constitutes correct actions was carefully elaborated in a system called *varnashrama-dharma*, "duties in accord with caste (*varna*) and stage of life (*ashrama*)."

Brahma Says

Varnashrama-dharma is duty according to caste and stage of life; **varna** is the four castes and **ashrama** is the stage of life. A caste is the Hindu idea that society should be divided into hereditary classes.

The basic idea of the caste system was evident as early as the Vedic hymn that described the four classes, or *varnas*, of society. But this system of four general classes was only the ideological framework for a much more complicated social hierarchy. The *varnas* are as follows:

- Priests
- Rulers/warriors

- Artisan/merchant/farmers
- Servants

Within the four castes (*varnas*), there developed a multitude of *jatis,* "birth groups." These were made up of communities that did not intermarry, most of them associated with specific occupations. There were *jatis* for weavers, carpenters, oil-pressers, goldsmiths, silversmiths, tinsmiths, temple priests, priests who performed Vedic rituals, and priests who taught. The hierarchy of these groups varied from one village to another. The weaver may have had a high status in one town and a low one in another.

In general, the status of a *jati* was determined by the type of work it did. Jobs that were ritually unclean, such as work requiring handling of the dead, whether in human funerary services or preparation of animal hides, had low status. There was also an economic component. A family that was wealthy could have a higher status in its community than poorer families with the same occupation in another area. But, high caste did not guarantee superior economic status.

In some villages, the wealthiest landowners are Shudras (the servant caste), and often Brahmins who served as temple priests in small communities were quite poor. The caste system organized society according to class and occupation, and your place in this system determined the way you were supposed to behave in society.

Men in the *Ashramas*

For men of the upper three castes, behavior was also regulated by your stage in life. There are four *ashramas* (stages in life):

- Student: The student's first teachers are the parents, and then formal education begins when the child is sent to study with a professional teacher who tailors the education to fit the family's social status.

- Householder: Now grown, you marry, raise a family, and work for the benefit of the family and to maintain your place in the community. When the children are grown and have begun to have their own offspring, you enter the third stage.

- Forest Dweller: The forest dweller lets the children take over the family business and starts to devote greater energy to spiritual concerns.

Bet You Didn't Know

The *sannyasin* performs his own funerary rites and takes a new name to separate himself from his old life. He may then live alone as a hermit or in a monastery where he devotes all his energy to meditation and religious activities.

- *Sannyasa:* This means complete renunciation, which is not for everyone. If you feel the desire to seek liberation from rebirth, you can leave the family, give up all social connections, and become an ascetic.

Women in the *Ashramas*

Women's lives were not organized into the same four stages as the men. Although records of female sages taking part in Upanishadic debates suggest that girls did go through a student stage in the Vedic age, by the first century women were not allowed to study the Vedas.

> **Hindu Hints**
>
> Most scholars believe that the inclusion of the *sannyasin* as a fourth stage was an attempt to prevent people from abandoning their social duties to take up the life of an ascetic. By advocating renunciation as a final stage of life, after all social obligations are completed, the ascetic tradition could be integrated into the larger social order. It is, however, notable that this program had limited success. Most people who feel a call to become renunciants do not wait until the last years of their lives to take up the ascetic life.

Householder life was considered the primary focus for women, so a girl's education was limited to the art of running a home. It is said that the marriage ceremony is a woman's equivalent to the ritual that marks a boy's entry into the formal student stage, serving her husband is like serving a guru (spiritual teacher), and household chores are her fire rituals. Women were supposed to accompany their husbands when the men entered the forest-dweller stage, but there is no textual evidence to suggest that women were encouraged to become renunciants or achieve spiritual knowledge on their own.

Tradition ...

Certain patterns of behavior are expected for each caste at each stage of life. A body of legal texts developed to regulate human behavior and define these expectations. These texts are not divinely revealed, like the Vedas. Instead they are considered *smriti*, "that which is remembered." In other words, they are supposed to be records of tradition. It is here in these legal texts that the philosophical ideals intersect with daily life. These texts define the proper dharmic life; they explain how to perform the correct duties for your caste and stage in life. So, for example, the texts describe the proper age for a child to be sent to a teacher and what subjects he should learn.

The lore taught was supposed to be appropriate to the caste. A Brahmin studied the Vedas and ritual practices. If the lad was a Kshatriya (the warrior caste), after a brief introduction to the Vedas, he was to learn weaponry and statecraft. Women and Shudras (the servant caste) were not eligible even to hear the Vedas, so they were excluded from the educational system. This also meant that Shudras were excluded from the brahmanical religious system because they were not schooled in language and rituals.

Because the texts were written by the Brahmins, the concerns of the priests were treated in the greatest detail. Later materials also addressed issues of state and considered how laws should be applied to different levels of society. In the system that emerged, some punishments were much more severe for the lower castes than for the elites. It was a greater crime for a servant to kill a priest than for a priest to kill a servant. Conversely, however, higher castes were fined more severely for theft. A Shudra had to pay eight times the amount stolen, a Vaishya paid 16 times the amount, a Kshatriya paid 32 times the amount, and a Brahmin 64 times the amount stolen. According to one legal text, those who were educated were expected to adhere to higher standards of conduct.

The legal code laid out in these texts should be taken with a grain of salt. Although it purported to apply to everyone, it was essentially a code for the upper three castes. Most scholars believe the lower levels of society operated under their own codes. It was only in the modern period, when the British adopted these ancient texts as an India-wide legal system, that the upper-caste code was applied to all Hindus. Although the legal texts reflect brahmanical ideals rather than observations of reality, they also show the development of a concern with virtuous behavior defined by caste and stage in life.

The same criticism that prevents us from accepting the legal codes at face value must be leveled at all the textual material from the Vedic and Upanishadic period—these are the texts of an elite class and do not tell us about the religious lives of the majority of the people. This lopsided situation begins to change in the next period.

The great epics, the *Ramayana* and the *Mahabharata*, seem to have more relation to popular traditions and show how the brahmanical system was expanded to incorporate the beliefs and practices of the people. Popular beliefs and practices are even more evident in the Puranas, the vast body of literature that developed after the epics, and the collections of poetry and song drawn from the medieval devotional movement. The next chapter examines the interweaving of priestly and popular traditions.

The Least You Need to Know

- The Upanishads reflect an era of intense philosophical speculation, the material is mainly in the form of scholarly debates and teacher-student dialogues.

- The Upanishads devoted great energy to discussing the relationship between the external, cosmic aspect of *Brahman* and its internal aspect, usually called *atman*.

- According to the system of *samsara*, at death you would pass on to a life in heaven or hell, depending on the merits of your activities in life. Then, after a certain amount of time, the individual would be reborn on earth once again.

- Yoga includes moral, physical, and mental discipline because the body must be controlled before it is possible to control and focus the mind to reach higher knowledge.

- The definition of what constitutes correct actions was carefully elaborated in a system called *varnashrama-dharma*, which consisted of duties in accord with *varna* (the four levels of the caste system) and *ashrama* (the different stages of life).

Chapter 4

The Epic Period

In This Chapter

- The *Mahabharata* poem
- The *Ramayana* poem
- Dharma, dharma, it's everywhere
- Discipline of knowledge, action, and devotion

During the last centuries before the Common Era, Hinduism was less visible than Buddhism and Jainism in India. The rulers of the Mauryan Empire (c. 324–185 B.C.E.) had supported Buddhism, and other kings in subsequent kingdoms also patronized the Buddhist and Jain monks. There are extensive records of donations made to Buddhist and Jain monasteries by the members of the upper classes in this era, but there is little evidence for support of the Brahmins (priests). Then, beginning around 100 B.C.E., the Brahmins regained popularity by combining Upanishadic philosophy with folk religion.

The merger of priestly and popular traditions is evident in the epics and the Puranas. The epics are the two great poems, the *Mahabharata* and the *Ramayana*. The *Mahabharata* was compiled between 400 B.C.E. and 300 C.E., and the *Ramayana* was compiled between 200 B.C.E. and 200 C.E. Both are complex texts that incorporate diverse myths, legends, and philosophies within the framework of one extended narrative.

Brotherly Love, or Lack Thereof

The *Mahabharata*, which has approximately 100,000 verses, is the longest epic poem in the world. It contains a multitude of legends and lore all incorporated into a unifying narrative about a war for the rulership of north India. This core plot involves the descendants of two brothers. The elder brother, Dhritarashtra, was blind and therefore had been passed over for the rule of their father's kingdom, but later when the younger brother, Pandu, died, the elder became king. Because both brothers had ruled, the descendants of both claimed to be the legitimate successors.

The conflict of the *Mahabharata* centers on the power struggle between these two groups of cousins. The story is told from the perspective of the Pandavas, the five sons of Pandu: Yudhishtira, Bhima, Arjuna, Nakula, and Sahadeva. They are in opposition to the hundred Kauravas, led by Duryodhana. When the Pandavas challenge Duryodhana's right to rule, old Dhritarashtra tries to mediate peace by dividing the kingdom in two. He gives the rule of the northern area to Duryodhana and the southern area to Yudhishtira. There is peace until Duryodhana visits the south and falls into a palace pond, causing Yudhishtira to laugh at him.

Feeling insulted, Duryodhana challenges his cousin to a game of dice. Yudhishtira has a weakness for gambling and loses his entire kingdom, including Draupadi, the common wife of the Pandavas. The Kauravas try to humiliate Draupadi by stripping off her sari, but she prays to the god Krishna for aid, and the cloth becomes endless. Then the men play one final round of dice, with the understanding that the losers will go into exile for 12 years and spend a thirteenth year incognito or forfeit their kingdom. Yudhishtira loses again and the Pandavas, with Draupadi, go to the forest.

The 12 years in the forest bring many adventures and plenty of opportunity to work other stories into the larger narrative. During their exile, the Pandavas receive special teachings from saints and deities and acquire special powers, like the use of magical weapons and yogic abilities, through ascetic practices, study with sages, and boons from gods. They return to claim their kingdom at the end of the thirteenth year, but Duryodhana refuses to give it back so the cousins engage in a great civil war.

The Pandavas win but are distraught at the bloodshed and the loss of family and friends. After all, the two sets of cousins had grown up in the same palace and the people marshaled on both sides of the war were all known to each other. Yudhishtira turns over the rule of the kingdom to a young relative and the five brothers, with their wife, head for Indra's heaven in the Himalayas.

On the Right Path

Much of the epic poems are, undoubtedly, from popular traditions. Scholars theorize that the core narrative of the *Ramayana* began as a ballad sung by wandering bards as entertainment for royal assemblies. These stories gained authority as religious texts believed to recount the deeds of the gods themselves in human form.

Human and Demon Conflicts

The *Ramayana* is only about one quarter the length of the *Mahabharata*. It too concerns a struggle for rule of an earthly kingdom, but this time the conflict is between humans and demons.

Dasharatha, king of Ayodhya, has three wives who bear him four sons: Rama, Lakshmana, Shatrughuna, and Bharata. Rama is the eldest and is supposed to be his father's heir, but the youngest wife schemes to have her boy become king. She reminds Dasharatha that he once promised her a favor when she saved his life and demands that the favor be fulfilled by making her son king and banishing Rama for 14 years. The king must keep his word, and Rama even encourages him to do so because it is the right thing to do.

Rama, his wife Sita, and his brother Lakshmana go to live in the forest, and the old king dies of grief. Bharata, the brother who thus receives the throne, was not a party to the wheeling and dealing and is quite unhappy when he comes home and finds out what has happened. He goes to the forest and begs Rama to return, but Rama insists on staying in the forest to fulfill his father's vow. Bharata then goes home to Ayodhya, places Rama's sandals on the throne, and rules as regent until his brother can return.

Meanwhile Ravana, the 10-headed demon king of Lanka, manages to kidnap Sita from Rama's hut in the forest and carry her away to his home. Rama gathers an army of bears and monkeys to help fight the demons. His greatest aide is Hanuman, the monkey general who is the son of the wind god. Hanuman discovers where Sita is being held. Rama's army builds a bridge across the ocean to Lanka and successfully defeats the demons. Sita is rescued, but before Rama will take her back she is required to prove that she has remained chaste during her captivity. She does this by walking unharmed through a fire. Thereafter Rama and his family return to Ayodhya where the king's strict adherence to *dharma* ensures a golden age for his people.

Dharma: A Consistent Theme

Dharma is a prominent theme in both epics. The *Mahabharata* illustrates the difficulties that arise when *dharma* seems contrary to expectations of good and bad conduct. Adherence to filial duty causes Draupadi to become the wife of all five Pandavas. Arjuna comes home and calls to his

mother, Kunti, to come see what he has won in a
contest. His mother, with her back to him, says
that he must share his winnings with his brothers.
The prize is Draupadi. Kunti cannot take back her
injunction so her sons all agree to share Draupadi,
if the scheme is acceptable to her.

A more difficult lesson in *dharma* occurs at the
end of the *Mahabharata*, when Yudhishtira arrives
in heaven. There he finds Duryodhana, his great
enemy, enjoying celestial rewards because he has
fulfilled his *dharma* as a warrior. While Duryodhana has completed his duties in the mortal realm,
Yudhishtira is fated to be reborn one last time to
overcome the last vestiges of attachment that bind
him. This attachment was evidenced when he re-
fused to enter heaven unless the dog that had
become his companion was also admitted. The
dog turned out to be the god Dharma himself.

In the *Ramayana*, Rama places honor and duty
above all other considerations when he insists on
adhering to his father's vow and accepts his exile.
Sita is a model of wifely dharma, following him
into exile and keeping the thought of him before
her as a shield for her chastity throughout her
imprisonment.

The Bhagavad Gita

The issue of how to reconcile apparent contradictions in dharma and apply it to daily life is the

focus of the *Bhagavad Gita*. The *Bhagavad Gita* is part of the *Mahabharata*. The text is a dialogue between Arjuna, the greatest warrior among the Pandavas, and the god Krishna, also honored for his martial skills.

Krishna has taken the role of Arjuna's charioteer, and just before the battle commences, Arjuna and Krishna drive out into the battlefield and survey the armies lined up against each other. Arjuna looks at the two armies and sees relatives and friends amassed on both sides. He realizes that he will be forced to kill those he loves and, falling into despair, throws down his bow. Krishna tries to convince him that it is his duty to fight, but Arjuna can see no way to balance the necessity of carrying out his duty with the necessity of avoiding the sin of killing his relatives and respected teachers. Then Krishna begins to teach Arjuna how to live a dharmic life.

First Krishna teaches that the body is not the self, so that which is killed is not really the person. The true self is the eternal *atman*, which cannot be killed. It merely inhabits the body, like a suit of clothes, and then casts that body off at death and takes on another body at the time of rebirth. This goes on, lifetime after lifetime, until the self is liberated from the cycle of rebirth. In the *Bhagavad Gita*, Krishna outlines three paths that lead to this liberation:

1. The discipline of knowledge, *jnana-yoga*.

2. The discipline of action, *karma-yoga*.

3. The discipline of devotion, *bhakti-yoga*.

The Discipline of Knowledge

The discipline of knowledge is essentially the tradition of the Upanishads. This knowledge is an understanding of the true nature of the self as the *atman*, which has the same characteristics as Brahman.

> ### On the Right Path
>
> The wise person, who knows the *atman*, is serene because he is free of desires. He has no attachments and no fears. He is not affected by either pleasure or pain since both are aspects of one reality.

The Discipline of Action

The path of action requires that you fulfill your duties according to *varnashrama-dharma*, but do so without attachment to the results of your actions. In other words, actions should be carried out without fear of punishment or hope of reward, but merely because of duty. Arjuna's attempt to abandon his prescribed actions, his warrior's duty to fight, is not the correct solution to the problem of incurring *karman* through actions. You cannot simply refuse to carry out your duty.

Krishna points out that he, himself, is the supreme deity who creates and maintains the cosmos. If he ceased his actions, the universe would no longer exist. In the same way, all people must carry out the actions appropriate to their *dharma*. But those actions should be performed without desire for their fruits. If the actions are performed without desire, they do not produce binding *karman*. The easiest way to achieve this detachment is to offer all actions to Krishna. Then you may become a perfect person who does work in the interest of *lokasangraha*, "the good of the world."

Throughout the text, Krishna's teachings incorporate religious practices into daily life. The actions that lead to liberation are not just sacrificial rituals, any daily activity can be offered to Krishna. What matters is the attitude with which the actions are performed, not the type of activity. In this way, the benefits of religious practices are made accessible to non-Brahmins. You do not need to perform sacrificial rituals or spend years in meditation to attain liberation. Instead, by offering your actions to God, ordinary work becomes a sacrificial ritual. The activity of ritual behavior is internalized and equated with all daily activities.

The Discipline of Devotion

The *Bhagavad Gita* goes on to describe a third path, *bhakti-yoga*, the way of devotion. The path of knowledge requires time and training and can only be followed under the tutelage of a teacher. It is too difficult for untrained non-Brahmins, even if they have the resources. But the path of devotion is a householder path, accessible to all people, even the women and Shudras (servants) excluded from participation in Vedic religion.

> ## Hindu Hints
>
> Sincere devotion to Krishna super-sedes all knowledge and even actions. It is said that even an evildoer may achieve liberation if he worships Krishna with undivided devotion, because this worship will cause him to become virtuous and lead him to eternal peace. If the devotee makes Krishna the focus of every moment of life, he is liberated from the bonds of *karman*.

Bhakti-yoga is very similar to *karma-yoga*—both describe ways to make daily life a path to liberation. Furthermore the state of liberation to be achieved is a state of knowledge, so all three paths overlap. The different teachings are not exclusive, but alternate ways to attain a common goal.

In the *Bhagavad Gita*, Krishna's teachings incorporate the lifestyles of different levels of society into the larger pattern of *dharma*. In one passage, Krishna tells Arjuna it is better to do your own duty imperfectly than to perform another person's duty well (18.47). The text outlines the basic *dharma* of the different castes, but it is notable that the duties of Brahmins and Kshatriyas (warrior class) are described in detail while there is less said about the Vaishyas (the merchant/artisan/farming caste) and the only duty assigned to the Shudras is to serve (18.41–44). Still the text offers a model for including diverse groups within one system that is consistent with later Hindu inclusivism.

The characteristic that sets *bhakti-yoga* apart from *jnana-yoga* and *karma-yoga* is the relationship between the devotee and God. In the path of devotion, Krishna takes on the role of savior. The devotee makes progress through personal effort, but Krishna also helps out. He liberates people from bondage through divine grace and ensures them eternal peace. Krishna is a personal savior deity and, at the same time, is identified with the impersonal Brahman. In the *Bhagavad Gita*, the impersonal Absolute of the Upanishadic philosophers is blended with the theism of popular religious practice.

During the last century before the Common Era, the Brahmins began to emerge from their obscurity as the priests of a modified tradition. This new tradition interwove threads of priestly ritual practices, popular devotion to gods and goddesses, and the meditative practices of ascetic renunciation. Knowledge of these strands of tradition comes from four remarkable bodies of literature: the great epics, the Puranas, the Tantras, and the songs of the poet-saints. The result of this blending process was the colorful tapestry of classical and medieval Hinduism, the topics of the next chapter.

The Least You Need to Know

- The *Mahabharata* contains a multitude of legends and lore all incorporated into a unifying narrative about a war for the rulership of north India between the descendants of two brothers.

- The *Ramayana* is only about one quarter the length of the *Mahabharata* and also concerns a struggle for rule of an earthly kingdom, but the conflict is between humans and demons.

- The issue of how to reconcile apparent contradictions in *dharma* and apply it to daily life is the focus of the *Bhagavad Gita*, which is a dialogue between Arjuna, the greatest warrior among the Pandavas, and the god Krishna.

- The path of knowledge requires time and training and can only be followed under the tutelage of a teacher. The path of action requires that you fulfill your duties according to *varnashrama-dharma*. The path of devotion is a householder path, accessible to all people.

Chapter 5

Classical and Medieval Theism

In This Chapter

- Ancient books of the classical and medieval period
- Vishnu, the kingly god
- Shiva, a deity of paradoxes
- The Supreme Goddess, Devi
- Liberating knowledge through yogic practices

The era following the Epic Period is considered the Classical Age of Indian civilization. During this age, the Gupta dynasty established an empire that controlled most of north India and culturally influenced the southern kingdoms as well. The Gupta Period, dated from approximately 320–500 C.E., marks the reemergence of Hinduism as the dominant tradition of South Asia.

State sponsorship of Hinduism led to the development of great temples in the urban centers and support for the elaboration of scholarship related to religion. Sophisticated systems of astrology and astronomy were developed to calculate the ritual calendar. The necessity for precise transmission and recitation of the *shruti* texts led to the formation of material on grammar, etymology, phonetics, and metrics.

Schools of philosophy theorized about cosmology, human and divine natures and the relation between them, the modes of knowledge that create ignorance and bondage, and the ways to reach higher knowledge and liberation. Other cultural areas also developed in relation to religion. Medical lore was based on scriptural ideas about the correlation between the human body and the cosmos. Art, music, dance, and drama focused on myth and ritual. Temple architecture took on new forms and meanings.

The primary characteristic defining this classical Hinduism is its theism, a theism that pervaded public ritual and ascetic practices. In public rituals, the great temples were centers for worship of deities that had been brought within the sphere of brahmanical authority. These were local deities that had become universal gods through identification with Brahman. Among ascetic traditions, theism merged with *yoga* to form the esoteric systems known as Tantrism.

Ideas from Tantrism were then popularized and reabsorbed into mainstream devotional traditions.

New theological systems developed to synthesize Upanishadic philosophy with medieval devotion and *yoga*. Then in the later medieval period when north India was ruled by Muslims, the locus of Hindu vitality shifted to poet-saints who inspired a devotional movement that transcended traditional ritualism and emphasized personal experiences of divinity.

Theism in the Puranas

The Puranas, the "ancient" books of the classical and medieval period, are compendiums of myth, legend, and history that reflect popular theistic traditions. There are 18 great Puranas that are considered scripture by most Hindus, and many lesser Puranas with regional authority.

On the Right Path

Some schools of Hinduism consider the Puranas to be *shruti* (revelation) just like the Vedas. The Puranas together with the epics are often called the Fifth Veda, and because these texts have been available to all people, regardless of caste, they are actually much more influential than the original four Vedas.

Unlike the Vedas, the Puranas were never codified for use in rituals. They were passed down as oral traditions, with numerous local variations, and were written down at different times and places, in both Sanskrit and vernacular versions. The materials within individual Puranas show evidence of interpolations and additions that make it nearly impossible to assign clear dates to the texts. In general, the bulk of the material was probably established by the end of the Gupta Period (c. 500 C.E.) but additions continued long after. A broad date for the 18 great Puranas would be from 400–1000 C.E.

Five Topics and Four Aims

According to tradition, Puranas have five topics:

- The creation of the world
- The dissolution of the world
- The ages of the world
- Genealogies
- Stories about the descendants of the dynasties described in the genealogies

In fact, these topics make up only a fraction of the Puranic material. Other topics receiving greater attention include the four aims of life (that is wealth, enjoyment, social duty, and liberation from rebirth), religious observances (*vratas*), rites for dead ancestors (*shraddha*), descriptions of places of pilgrimage (*tirthas*), gifts/charity (*dana*), means of subsistence, manifestations of higher beings, and Brahman as the underlying support of the cosmos. These texts provide a window into the actual religious life of Hinduism, in all its rich complexity and myriad manifestations.

Purana Deities

Each Purana tends to focus on a specific deity as the Supreme Being responsible for creating and ordering the world. Myths about gods explain the origins of sacred places and rituals.

Hindu Hints

Philosophical descriptions of proper modes of behavior and goals in life are reported as conversations, between sages and deities or even among the gods themselves. Gods and goddesses discuss how you should perform rituals of worship and the mental attitudes that lead to spiritual goals like liberation from rebirth.

The theism that dominates the Puranas was not new. Some of the Upanishads had equated Brahman with specific deities. In the *Bhagavad Gita*, however, Krishna is a savior deity as well as the god who creates and manages the cosmos. Krishna's role as savior is made explicit when he says that he enters the world for the sake of his devotees.

> Whenever a decrease of righteousness exists, Arjuna, and there is a rising up of unrighteousness, then I manifest Myself. For the protection

of the good and the destruction of evil doers, for the sake of establishing righteousness, I am born in every age. (*BhG.* 4.7–8)

In this passage, Krishna explains what became the *avatara* doctrine. The word avatara means "a descent, an incarnation." Whenever there is trouble in the world, God takes on a physical form and descends into the world to reestablish order. Thus Krishna is not just Arjuna's charioteer, he is a form of the supreme God who creates, maintains, and destroys the universe.

In the *Bhagavad Gita*, Arjuna is permitted to glimpse Krishna's cosmic form. He sees the entire universe, the sun, stars, planets, and all the people gathered on the battlefield within the body of Krishna. Krishna tells him that everything that exists is part of himself, but that he is not limited to everything that exists. In other words, just as the Vedic Purusha extended 10 finger-lengths beyond the created universe, so too Krishna is the entire cosmos and more. As an *avatara* of the Supreme, the deity is simultaneously the transcendent Brahman and the immanent Krishna. This brings brahmanical philosophy together with popular theism.

Equating a deity with Brahman naturally makes that deity supreme. But there were many gods and goddesses in South Asia and people did not simply give up their local traditions because they adopted a belief in one supreme Principle. Instead, Hinduism developed ways to include multiple divinities within the brahmanical philosophy. Thus different deities came to be seen as manifestations of the one Supreme. The one Brahman took on all the diverse forms of the manifest universe and that included the various gods and goddesses found in regional traditions. This system of multiple divine forms extended beyond the gods to include sacred images, scriptures, and saints.

Three basic traditions emerged, defined by the deity identified as the one Supreme from which came all the other gods and goddesses.

- Those who consider Vishnu the highest god are called Vaishnavas.
- Those who name Shiva as Supreme are the Shaivas.
- The devotees of Devi, the Goddess, are called Shaktas because the energy that manifests as the cosmos is the feminine Shakti.

These three great deities, who dominate the Puranic literature and are the focus of Hinduism from the classical age to modern times, are covered in the sections that follow.

Vishnu

Of the three great deities, Vishnu fits into brahmanical philosophy most easily. Vishnu is described as a kingly god who is greatly concerned with *dharma*. He is irrevocably associated with *avatara* doctrine.

Vishnu enters the world in order to preserve order whenever unrighteousness threatens. The idea of successive incarnations allowed Vishnu to absorb other deities, thus bringing different religious traditions together in one system.

So, for example, Vishnu incarnated as a dwarf in the Vedas to reclaim the universe from the demons who had dispossessed the gods. The number of incarnations varies from one Purana to another, but the most popular tradition gives 10 *avataras*. Of these, Krishna and Rama, the heroes who ensure the triumph of *dharma* in the *Mahabharata* and the *Ramayana*, are the most widely revered.

Vishnu's manifestation is not, however, limited to *avataras*. According to the Vaishnava creation story, all the deities come from Vishnu. Vishnu is Brahman, the cause and substance of the cosmos.

On the Right Path

Vishnu is both the conscious *purusha* and the material *prakriti*, the two primordial principles of Samkhya philosophy (refer to Chapter 3), and he is also time (*kala*) which brings about the connection and separation of *purusha* and *prakriti*.

In the old Samkhya theory, the primordial principles were ultimately separate, but in the Puranas, they are all part of the infinite Vishnu. Creation begins when Vishnu disturbs the equilibrium of the three qualities (*gunas*) of *prakriti*, thereby causing *prakriti* to evolve the elements of existence. These elements come together to form a vast egg resting on the cosmic waters. Vishnu enters this world-egg as the creator god, Brahma, and arranges creation. Then he takes the role of Vishnu the preserver and maintains order in the cosmos. Finally he becomes Shiva the destroyer and dissolves his creation into a great ocean.

Vishnu then sleeps on the waters until it is time for a new creation. The image of the god sleeping on a serpent that floats on the ocean is often depicted in Hindu art. Creation recommences when a lotus grows from Vishnu's navel and Brahma emerges from the blossom to create the worlds once again. This is a secondary level of creation since the destruction of the cosmos did not revert all the way back to unified *prakriti*.

Within these periods of activity and rest there are smaller cycles of creation. The smallest cycle is made up of four ages. The first age is an idyllic period when dharma is strong, but in the subsequent periods *dharma* declines. The fourth period is called the Kali Yuga, the Dark Age, in which *dharma* is weakest and people fail to follow their duties or even strive for virtue. The world is currently in a Kali Yuga that began in 3102 B.C.E. When *dharma* is entirely depleted, the world is destroyed and recreated so a new Golden Age begins.

The four ages together, called a *manvantara* or "life of Manu," last 4,320,000 years. A thousand of these manvantaras make up a day of Brahma. Each day is followed by a night of Brahma, during which Vishnu sleeps. One day and one night make up a *kalpa*. Then Vishnu awakes and there is a new kalpa. After 100 years of 360 days and nights, the entire process of creation reverses until Vishnu has reabsorbed *purusha, prakriti,* and time back into himself. The cyclic system of time experienced by people who are caught in the round of rebirth is magnified on the cosmic level.

Bet You Didn't Know

The Krishna of the Puranas bears little resemblance to the divine counselor of the *Bhagavad Gita*. Puranic stories focus on the infant Krishna who miraculously kills those sent to assassinate him, the mischievous child who leads the town children in and out of trouble, and the divine youth who enchants the *gopis* (milkmaids) with his flute music and dances with them in the forest.

The different *avataras* are thought to appear to meet the needs of specific eras. Vishnu incarnated as Rama in the previous age when there was still enough *dharma* to make his righteous rule feasible. Then, when the Dark Age began, religious practices were modified, so it was for this purpose that Vishnu took on the form of Krishna. He not only aided the Pandavas in the great war, he taught the path of devotion which is the way to salvation when there is so little *dharma* in the world that self-effort is no longer sufficient.

Shiva

Shaivas ascribe the supreme role to Shiva, and see Vishnu and all other deities as forms of their great god. Shiva has been described as a deity of paradoxes because he is simultaneously a renunciant and a householder, and a celibate *yogin* and a husband. This is not, however, a contradiction in the Hindu belief system since asceticism generates internal energy that is very closely related to sexual energy. The power of that energy may be both creative and destructive, and Shaivism emphasizes the awesome power and otherness of God by describing Shiva as both creator and destroyer. Several of the Shaiva sects follow practices that are not part of the brahmanical system. This, combined with clues found in the Shaiva myths, suggests that Shiva may be a non-Aryan deity.

Shiva did not play a role in the Vedic hymns, although he later became identified with the Vedic deity Rudra. Shiva is mentioned in some of the Upanishads and is described as the supreme deity, equated with Brahman as the source of the universe, in the *Shvetashvatara Upanishad*. He makes several appearances in the epics where he teaches, bestows knowledge, and rewards those who practice yogic austerities. It seems clear that the deity had a long history within non-brahmanical ascetic traditions, but was only grudgingly admitted to the mainstream. The reluctance to include Shiva in Brahmanism is illustrated by the story of Sati.

Sati was Shiva's wife and the daughter of Daksha. One day she learned that her father was going to hold a sacrificial ritual and had invited all the gods except Shiva. Humiliated by the neglect of her husband, she committed suicide through the fire of her yogic power. Shiva became enraged, took on a terrible form, destroyed the sacrifice, and killed Daksha. Then the god resurrected Daksha and the sacrifice, and the ritual proceeded with Shiva included this time.

In the Shaiva Puranas, Shiva is the Absolute, the God responsible for creation, preservation, and destruction of the cosmos. Parama Shiva (Supreme Shiva) creates by dividing into two aspects, the masculine Shiva and the feminine Shakti. Shakti, the active power of the divine, is the agent of creation. She becomes manifest in all the names and forms of the cosmos. The unification of these two aspects is illustrated in an image of Shiva with the right half of the deity's body male and the left female. Shiva and Shakti are also united in the Shiva *lingam*. Shiva lingam, a phallus that rests within a circular *yoni*, representing the female Shakti.

Brahma Says _____

Lingam is the nonrepresentational image of Shiva. Yoni is the nonrepresentational image of Devi.

Although Shiva is known as the destroyer and his ascetic tendencies are linked with fierce forms, there are also stories of his compassion and protection. When the gods and demons churned the ocean to obtain the nectar of immortality, they let loose a poison that threatened to destroy all life. Shiva swallowed the poison, which was so powerful that it stained his throat blue. Images of the god usually show this discoloration. Images also show a river flowing out of Shiva's matted hair. This is the river Ganges, which cascades from the heavens to the mortal world below. The waters would have destroyed the earth if they had fallen with their full force, so Shiva caught the river in his hair and dissipated the strength of its impact.

Shiva is also known as Nataraj, the Lord of the Dance. The image of the dancing god, so beautifully rendered in the bronze sculpture of the southern Chola kingdoms, is a compact treatise on Shaiva theology. It represents creation and destruction, control and abandon, and transcendence and immanence. Creation arises from the drum in one hand, a second hand makes a gesture of reassurance, promising protection, while a third hand carries the fire of destruction. Beneath the god's foot is a dwarf who represents cosmic evil and human weaknesses, both of which are overcome by the grace of Shiva. The dance itself has been called the dance of destruction. But, on the cosmic level, destruction is the prelude to recreation, and on the personal level, destruction is the means to remove the bonds that hold the devotee to the cycle of rebirth.

Devi

Although some female deities are revered in the Vedas, prior to the Puranas, there is little evidence for worship of a Goddess as the supreme deity. There are, however, many local goddesses mentioned in various texts and these were probably gradually incorporated into brahmanical tradition.

The earliest work to glorify the supreme Goddess was the *Devi Mahatmya*, compiled between the fifth and the seventh centuries C.E. In this text, the Goddess intervenes three times in order to destroy demons that threaten the world. First she prevents two demons from disrupting the process of creation. Her second appearance is the basis for one of the Goddess's most popular images, that of the female warrior Durga.

A demon named Mahisha is defeating the gods in battle, so the gods go to Shiva, Brahma, and Vishnu for help. When these deities hear what is happening, they become enraged. Then three lights spring from their angry faces and the lights merge to become a beautiful Goddess. This is Durga, who goes out to defeat Mahisha armed with weapons from each of the gods. The Goddess also has the ability to emanate other Goddesses from herself as when Durga becomes angry and her anger takes the form of the dark Goddess, Kali, who triumphs over another demon.

The third major intervention also takes place in battle when the Goddess as Ambika draws all her

divine multi-forms, including Kali, into herself in
order to slay the demons Shumbha and Nishumbha.
At the end of the text, the gods praise the Goddess
as the mother of the universe, and she promises to
protect her creation whenever necessary.

Once the idea of a supreme Goddess gained acceptance, all goddesses became forms of the One, Devi.
Devi is the active power, the *shakti*, that manifests
as the universe. She is the mother of everything but
she is not merely a soft, maternal figure. She is an
embodiment of both creative and destructive power.
She can be depicted as Lakshmi, the goddess of
good fortune, offering bounty, or as Kali, the dark
goddess of the battlefield, who drinks the blood of
her enemies.

Bet You Didn't Know

The girdle of severed arms the dark
Goddess wears around her waist represents the *karman* which she liberates her
devoted children from and the garland of
decapitated heads around her neck symbolizes human failings, such as greed and
lust, which she destroys so that her devotees may attain liberation.

These forms are not antithetical, they are two illus-
trations of Devi's power, representing both the gentle and fierce aspects with which she cares for the
world. As gentle Lakshmi, the goddess cares for her

devotees through worldly benefits. As fierce Kali, she destroys the enemies who threaten the world. The harmony of these two aspects is further evident in the way the devotees who address Kali as "Mother" allegorize her ferocious form.

Although all goddesses are theoretically included within Devi, the individual entities are worshiped in their own right as well. Two of the most popular goddesses are Sarasvati and Lakshmi. Sarasvati is known as the goddess of learning and is also a patroness of music. Dressed in white and riding a swan, she plays on a stringed instrument called a vina and carries a manuscript and string of beads. The manuscript ties her to scripture and in some traditions she is said to have created *devanagari*, the "divine script" in which Sanscrit is written.

Lakshmi is often depicted standing on a lotus flanked by elephants while gold coins shower from her hands. She is the goddess of good fortune who brings prosperity to her worshipers. Her image adorns modern Indian coins and Divali, the festival of lights, is held every year to invoke the goddess's aid.

One way in which the goddesses of South Asia are tied together is through a myth that gives a common origin to their sacred sites. In this story, Sati, wife of Shiva, dies as described earlier in the story of Shiva and Daksha. Grief-stricken, Shiva takes up her corpse and carries it about the world (India). His rampage causes cosmic disruption so Vishnu follows him and slices pieces from Sati's body until Shiva finds his hands empty and is able to put his grief aside and return to his mountain abode where he immerses himself in meditation. The places where the pieces of Sati's body fell to earth became sacred as shrines to various goddesses.

Hindu Hints

The story of Shiva and Daksha also shows the physical association between the goddess and the land of India, which, in modern times, has been personified as the deity Bharat Mata, Mother India.

Secondary Deities

There are numerous deities who are only loosely combined with Shiva, Vishnu, and Devi and really retain their own identities. One such is Ganesha, the elephant-headed god, who is the son of Parvati and stepson of Shiva. Ganesha is one of the most widely revered gods in India, and small images of him are found over the doors of many homes. He is known as the remover of obstacles so people make offerings to him before any new undertaking.

Another deity related to Shiva is Murukan, the most popular deity of the southern Tamil tradition. Although Murukan has a long history as a non-brahmanical war god, he became identified with Skanda, Shiva's son. The great festivals of south India are held in honor of this god. Hanuman, the monkey who aided Rama in the Ramayana, also developed a following. Hanuman is revered as a perfect exemplar of devotion.

There are, moreover, countless regional and village deities. Many of these are goddesses who serve as the protectors of specific villages. The village goddesses are usually represented in non-pictorial form, often by a pot of water, a tree or rock covered in red paint, or a thorn bush with strips of cloth tied to it. Villagers may recognize these deities as local manifestations of the great gods whose images reside in the temples, but mostly they approach them as independent powers.

A second category of local deity is made up of human beings who have been divinized. There are two types of people in this group, heroes and unhappy ghosts. The heroes are people who have lived extraordinary lives, especially lives of perfect *dharma*. The unhappy ghosts are people who died in bad circumstances. Such people become dangerous ghosts who linger near the living, causing harm. These spirits must be placated with offerings so they will turn away from malevolence.

Theism and Tantra

The power of ghosts and heroes reflects the correlation between humanity and divinity that pervades Hinduism. This correlation, which has its roots at least as far back as the *Purusha Sukta* of the *Rig Veda*, was elaborated in the texts called Tantras. Most of these texts are from the eighth century of the Common Era or later. In these texts, esoteric yogic philosophy is blended with popular theism. Out of this

comes a new set of practices that are then reabsorbed back into other traditions.

Tantrism elaborates ideas already seen in Samkhya
philosophy about attaining liberating knowledge
through yogic practices designed to reverse the
process of creation, but the interpretation of that
process is adapted to Puranic cosmology. Creation
is caused by the division of Brahman into two
aspects, one male and one female. These are identified with Shiva and Shakti by Shaiva or Shakta
Tantrics, known as Vishnu and Shri Lakshmi in
Shri Vaishnavism, and referred to as Krishna and
Radha in Gaudiya Vaishnavism.

Shakti, the female aspect, then unfolds into all the
forms of the cosmos. The process of creation passes
from an unmanifest state to subtle form and then
to material manifestation. In Tantrism, the unmanifest whole is often called Shabdabrahman,
Brahman as the Word, and the process of Shakti's
unfoldment is the process of subtle sound becoming audible sound.

The human body is a product of this process of
manifestation, just like the entire cosmos. Since
the Shakti that becomes the universe also becomes
the individual, the body is a microcosm of the universe, with subtle and material levels. It is thus
possible to retrace the process of creation within
the human body. Through this reversal of creation,
Shakti is reunified with Shiva and the individual
attains liberation from rebirth.

Tantrism develops precise descriptions of this process. Within the body, Shakti resides dormant at the base of the spine as the Kundalini energy. When the Kundalini is awakened, it rises up through the spinal column. It passes through specific centers within the body called *chakras*. The number of *chakras* varies among texts, but the classical description names six centers, each associated with specific letters of the alphabet and deities. Eventually the Kundalini-shakti reaches the crown of the head, the abode of Shiva, and the two merge once again as Brahman, the neuter, unmanifest Whole. As this process goes on, the student gains special powers of physical and mental control. He is also supposed to acquire magical abilities such as levitation.

Brahma Says _____

Chakra means "circle"; centers along the subtle spinal channel in Tantra.

This process requires careful discipline under the guidance of a qualified spiritual teacher, a guru, who tailors practices to the individual student. The guru derives his (or her) authority from personal spiritual attainment and the ability to help others achieve enlightenment. It is said that finding a qualified teacher who can lead you to realization is a marvel for among the few who possess the knowledge, only a handful have the disposition to teach. Such a person is revered above even God for it is by the grace of the guru that the devotee attains knowledge of the Lord. Tantric gurus belonged to teaching lineages and did not have to be Brahmins. Tantrism was open to men and women of all castes; the requirement for taking up the path was a sincere desire for liberation and initiation by a guru.

Tantric Schools

Tantrism developed two distinct schools—Left-handed Tantra and Right-handed Tantra. The Left-handed Tantra was completely outside the brahmanical tradition. This school utilized practices that went against the usual rules, to help students overcome limited perceptions about the nature of the self and the world.

The goal was to be like the person of wisdom espoused in the Upanishads and the *Bhagavad Gita*, a person who sees everything as Brahman and does not differentiate pleasure or pain. Such a person would be free from the restraints of societal norms. A system of breaking normal religious rules was used to purify the student. This involved ritual consumption of the forbidden substances, meat, fish, alcohol, and parched grain, and the practice of ritual intercourse. Normally these things were thought to inhibit religious attainment so the Tantric used them to learn true detachment.

The Right-handed school did not engage in these traditionally impure actions and advocated mental worship instead of external rituals.

Tantras and Yantras and Mantras, Oh My

Tantrism developed the use of *yantras* and mantras as tools of discipline. The idea of mantras can be traced back to the Vedas. A mantra is a sacred utterance—a verse, phrase, or word—imbued with power. In earlier times, these had come from the Vedas but now the mantras were related to the Puranic deities. So, for example, the great Shaiva mantra is *Om namah shivaya*, "Let there be obeisance to Shiva."

> **Brahma Says**
>
> **Yantra** is a diagram used to aid meditation. The patterns represent the cosmos and the process of creation.

Mantras were given to disciples by their gurus during initiation. A disciple might have heard a mantra before this ritual, but the utterance of the words by the teacher imbued them with power and made them an efficacious part of the spiritual path.

The *yantra* is a diagram that symbolizes the relation of Shiva and Shakti. At its center is a dot called a *bindu*, representing unmanifest unity. This is surrounded by interlocking triangles, those pointing down representing Shakti and those pointing up Shiva. Variations on this pattern add the letters of the alphabet and numerous deities considered as manifestations of aspects of Shiva-Shakti. The *yantra* is supposed to serve as a focus of meditation that draws the mind toward the unified center.

Brahma Says

Bindu is the point at the center of a **mandala,** which is a diagram used in meditation.

Very few Tantric groups exist in South Asia, and the membership within these groups is small, but Tantric ideas have become part of the mainstream. Use of mantras is especially widespread. The names of the gods have become mantras, imbued with all the power of the gods they identify. Devotees of Krishna who chant *Hare Rama Hare Krishna*, "hail Rama, hail Krishna," are reciting a mantra that is also a prayer. *Yantras*, also called *mandalas*, are widely used in meditation, are found in art, and are worked into the floor plans of temples.

The special powers that are supposed to develop as a side effect of Tantric practice are part of a wider belief that religious attainment brings special abilities. Even in the Vedas, a person with Vedic knowledge was described as having divine attributes. In the *Yoga Sutras*, the yogic adept had the same kind of powers as a Tantric. In village culture, yogins are often approached for help with daily problems. They are asked to help women conceive, to cure sickness, and even to bring rain in times of drought. In this way, the living adept has many of the same powers as the divine hero.

The Least You Need to Know

- The Puranas, the ancient books of the classical and medieval period, are compendiums of myth, legend, and history that reflect popular theistic traditions.

- Vishnu is forever associated with *avatara* doctrine. It is Vishnu who enters the world in order to preserve order whenever unrighteousness threatens.

- Shiva has been described as a deity of paradoxes because he is simultaneously a renunciant and a householder, and a celibate *yogin* and a husband.

- Although some female deities are revered in the Vedas, prior to the Puranas, there is little evidence for worship of a goddess as the supreme deity.

- Tantrism elaborates ideas already seen in Samkhya philosophy about attaining liberating knowledge through yogic practices designed to reverse the process of creation, but the interpretation of that process is adapted to Puranic cosmology.

Chapter 6

Vedanta Tradition and the Bhakti Movement

In This Chapter

- The synthesis of philosophy and devotion
- God's saving grace
- Islam and the Bhakti movement

Vedanta, the "end of the Vedas," is the name given to the most influential philosophy from the medieval period. There are actually several distinct schools within Vedanta, each with its own great teachers and doctrines. The core focus of these schools is the understanding of the relationship between Brahman and *atman*, based on interpretations of three works—the Upanishads, the *Bhagavad Gita*, and the *Brahma Sutras*. From here we move on to the *bhakti* movement, which came from the Tamil region of south India.

Philosophy and Devotion Synthesized

The *Brahma Sutras* (c. first century C.E.) contains approximately 500 aphorisms, which are supposed to summarize the wisdom of the Upanishads, but these terse statements are difficult to understand so the Vedantins interpreted them in relation to the other two texts.

Advaita Vedanta

The Vedanta tradition most familiar in the West is associated with Shankara (c. 788–820 C.E.), the philosopher who first put together a coherent inter-pretation of the texts that came to form the basis of Vedanta. Shankara's philosophy is called *Advaita Vedanta*, "non-dual Vedanta," because he described Brahman as non-dual. There is only one reality and that is Brahman. The individual *atman* is identical to Brahman (as taught in the Upanishads), but people see themselves as distinct entities in a world of di-verse forms because of *maya*, "illusion." When that illusion is pierced, you realize that there is nothing but Brahman. Then the cycle of rebirth ceases and, at death, the individual *atman* merges into Brahman.

Brahma Says

Advaita means non-duality and is the name of a school of Vedanta.

Shankara's path to liberation is essentially a *yoga* of knowledge. It is through knowledge of Brahman that illusion is overcome and realization achieved. The Brahman one realizes is infinite and attribute-less, as in the Upanishads. But there are also theistic Upanishads and Shankara synthesized them with his philosophy by describing two levels of Brahman:

- *Saguna* (with attributes)
- *Nirguna* (without attributes)

Saguna Brahman is Brahman with attributes, the personal Lord who creates, maintains, and destroys, the God who is the receiver of sacrifices and the object of devotion. This Lord is an appropriate focus for those who are not yet capable of comprehending the higher truth of the attribute-less Supreme, the nirguna Brahman. In this way, *karma-yoga* and *bhakti-yoga* are incorporated into Advaita Vedanta as preparatory stages that train the devotee for *jnana-yoga*.

On the Right Path

Shankara organized the Dashanami monastic order for his followers and established monasteries (called *maths*) where disciples could study his teachings. His followers traveled throughout South Asia to share their philosophy. The leaders of the Shankara *maths* are still among the most respected religious authorities in India.

Vishishta-advaita Vedanta

Shankara's system, which was not designed for house-holder life and demoted theistic devotion, is far less representative of majority Hinduism than the teachings of Ramanuja. Ramanuja (c. 1025–1137 C.E.) utilized the theism of the medieval literature in his interpretation of the Vedanta texts to formulate the school known as *Vishishta-advaita*, "qualified non-dualism." Here, the supreme Brahman is the personal Lord, in other words, Brahman with attributes.

> **Brahma Says**
>
> **Vishishta-advaita,** which means "qualified non-dualism" is the name of a school of Vedanta.

Brahman is the ground of existence, but individual souls and matter are eternally distinct parts of Brahman. So, although Brahman is everything, and therefore non-dual, that non-dualism is qualified by the distinct existence of souls and matter.

Because souls and matter exist eternally within Brahman, the world is real and souls retain their individuality even in liberation. The individual souls are caught in *samsara* because of ignorance and *karman*. This bondage can be overcome by means of three types of effort:

1. Action with detachment.
2. Study of Vedanta to understand the nature of God, soul, and matter.
3. Devotion (*bhakti*).

Ramanuja describes this devotion as self-surrender and constant contemplation of God. These three activities lead to the highest *bhakti*, which is the immediate, intuitive knowledge of Brahman.

This Brahman is a personal God possessed of perfect attributes such as omniscience and omnipotence. The liberated soul, freed of all ignorance and negative *karman*, becomes similar to Brahman and dwells in eternal, blissful communion with the Lord. There must be a distinction between the soul and God to make this relationship possible.

Ramanuja's school reverses the hierarchy of *saguna* and *nirguna* established by Shankara. Here the experience of the *atman* merging into the attributeless Brahman (which is the highest attainment of Advaita Vedanta) is a preliminary stage of purification before the self regains a sense of personal identity and passes on to attain a higher stage of permanent communion with the personal Lord. This qualified non-dualism is much closer to householder and temple Hinduism than the monastic philosophy of Shankara. Ramanuja's theology synthesized Upanishadic philosophy with the experience of devotion to a personal God made popular by the great poet-saints of south India.

Ramanuja's philosophy reflects the powerful influence of devotion in the development of medieval and modern Hinduism. The *bhakti* (devotional) movement began in south India in the sixth century of the Common Era and spread north. This movement came out of the religious experiences of poet-saints who traveled from one holy site to another, singing hymns to gods. The saints came from all levels of society, included women as well as men, and used vernacular languages instead of Sanskrit to express their devotion. They were, therefore, part of the popular religious world, not the elite priesthood. Yet their impact was so great that even the Brahmin theologians acknowledged them as ideal devotees, and their songs were incorporated into temple liturgies. Thus the devotional poems were blended with priestly traditions so that the experiences of poet-saints influenced theological interpretations like the works of Ramanuja.

Early Bhakti Movement

There were two early groups of poet-saints:

- The 12 Alvars who sang about Vishnu and his *avataras* from the sixth to the ninth centuries.

- The 63 Nayanars who lauded Shiva from the sixth to the twelfth centuries.

Both of these groups were in south India, but their influence spread throughout the subcontinent.

A primary theme in the works of the Alvars was God's saving grace. Their songs describe Vishnu's efforts to aid people by entering the world as an *avatara* or taking up residence in a temple image. They frequently sang of Vishnu as Krishna, but their emphasis was on Krishna as the beloved, young cowherd rather than the awesome teacher of the *Bhagavad Gita*. Often the Alvars would describe themselves as the *gopis*, the milkmaids who longed for Krishna's presence. Intense longing for a vision of the Lord reverberates through their poetry. These poems were collected together in the eleventh century and are considered revealed, like the Vedas, in the Shri Vaishnava tradition.

The Nayanars followed a similar path. They came from all levels of society, from Shudra to Brahmin, included both men and women, and expressed their devotion in the Tamil language that could be understood and sung by everybody. Like those of the Alvars, their songs expressed emotional relationships with a personal God, not an abstract, attributeless Brahman. These hymns too were collected and became part of the theological basis for later Shaiva sects, especially the Shaiva Siddhanta.

Late Medieval Bhakti

A second great wave of devotionalism emerged in northern India beginning in the thirteenth century. The two great influences on Hinduism in northern India during the later medieval period were Islam and this *bhakti* movement. Muslim raiders began to make their presence felt early in the eleventh century. In the year 1211, the establishment of the Delhi Sultanate marked the beginning of Muslim rule over large areas of north India.

Islam and Hinduism were not well suited to peaceful interaction, but the Muslims were outnumbered and did not make sustained attempts to counteract the indigenous religion. This relative tolerance ended during the reign of the Mughals, from 1526 to 1757. During the Mughal Period many of the Hindu temples in northern and western India were destroyed. In the midst of this era of social and political tension, popular Hindu saints celebrated the importance of personal religious experiences of devotion in marvelous vernacular prose and poetry.

Hindu Hints

Most of these poet-saints lived in northern and western India between the thirteenth and seventeenth centuries. Some of them attracted large groups of followers, several of which continue as distinct Hindu sects even today.

Like the earlier Tamil saints, the northerners came from all social classes and both genders, they came from different sects and revered different deities, but they shared a personal experience of the presence of the divine in the world. That presence took two distinct forms in the songs of the saints. Some of the poets emphasized the personal nature of God, describing divine attributes in great detail, while others extolled God as the formless Absolute. The former are called *saguna bhaktas*, "those who love a God with attributes," and the latter are *nirguna bhaktas*, "those who love an attributeless God." Often, one poet-saint vacillated between these two conceptions of the divine.

When the deity was described in personal terms, God's form was frequently the image from the local temple. The saints experienced the divine presence in the *murti*, the temple icon, and they celebrated the personal religion of devotion. Their songs describe their experiences of God, their local temples, and the importance of pilgrimage.

> **Brahma Says**
>
> **Murti** is the embodiment of the divine in an image. In stories about local saints, sometimes the *murti* comes to life and interacts with the devotee, perhaps going to meet him when he cannot come to the temple or allowing the saint to merge into the image and disappear from the mortal world.

The theism that permeated Hinduism in the classical period is still alive and well in the modern tradition. During the medieval period, theism combined with yogic practices and elaborate correlations between humanity and divinity in Tantra and synthesized with Upanishadic philosophy in Vedantin theology.

The clearest voice of Hindu theism came from the poet-saints, whose works were so influential that they became part of temple liturgy and shaped philosophy. By the late medieval period, all these strands had become entangled so that Tantric subtle-body imagery could appear in the poetry of an uneducated weaver and a Brahmin-poet could reject rituals and caste and tell everyone that the only religious practice necessary is to repeat the name of God with true devotion. The public and private practices that make up Hindu religious life solidified during the medieval period and have remained fairly constant up to modern times.

The Least You Need to Know

- The Vedanta tradition most familiar in the West is associated with Shankara (c. 788–820 C.E.), the philosopher who first put together a coherent interpretation of the texts that came to form the basis of Vedanta.

- Ramanuja (c. 1025–1137 C.E.) utilized the theism of the medieval literature in his interpretation of the Vedanta texts to formulate the school known as *Vishishta-advaita*, "qualified non-dualism."

- A primary theme in the works of the Alvars was God's saving grace. Their songs describe Vishnu's efforts to aid people by entering the world as an *avatara* or taking up residence in a temple image.

- The two great influences on Hinduism in northern India during the later medieval period were Islam and the *bhakti* movement.

- The theism that permeated Hinduism in the classical period is still alive and well in the modern tradition.

Temple Worship

In This Chapter

- Permanent temples as centers of worship
- Images of and in the temple

The main patterns of modern Hindu practice remain consistent with the religious life described in the Puranas. Renouncers meditate and cultivate detachment from the social world, priests chant and make offerings, and householders perform public and private worship. This public worship is the focus of this chapter. The private worship of deities will be covered in the next chapter.

Temple Architecture

One of the great contrasts between the ancient Vedic tradition and Hinduism is the localization of religion when permanent temples were established as centers of worship. The Vedic rituals were portable, they could be performed wherever a fire altar was properly built. By the classical period

(c. 320–500 C.E.), however, temples had become the focus of rituals, and instead of gods who resided in the atmosphere and must be worshiped through the intermediary of the fire that carried offerings up to the heavens, the gods were now established in specific locations.

Today these temples are the abodes of deities, places where the divine is immanent in the mortal world. Each temple has a presiding god or goddess, often accompanied by other associated deities, and usually a temple creation story tells how that deity came to reside in that place. In this way, the land of India is the land where the deities have manifested themselves.

Prior to the twentieth century, temples were usually built and supported by sponsorship from royalty and wealthy patrons. Patrons would make gifts of money, jewels, produce, and land. Because of this, popular temples often became well endowed. Large temples still have extensive land holdings and receive gifts from devotees. In modern times, temple funds are used to support charitable institutions, educational establishments, and hospitals. Some of the temples in India also sponsor the construction of temples in foreign countries for Hindus living outside of South Asia.

There is great regional diversity in Hindu temple architecture, but the structures can be categorized according to two general types of blueprints, a southern and a northern style. In both, the temple layout has correlations to the cosmos and to the divine body. The southern style has a central shrine set in an open courtyard. This is surrounded by a wall with four gates surmounted by towers, called *gopurams*, set at the cardinal points.

> ### Brahma Says
>
> A **gopuram** is a gate-tower for a south Indian temple. It is usually shaped in stepped layers, with images of deities decorating each level. These towers can be enormous, rising more than 200 feet in the air.

Larger temples are like small cities. The devotee passes through the gate into the inner yard and there finds small shrines to various deities surrounding the central shrine to the main presiding god or goddess. The layout is linked to the pattern of the *yantra* described earlier, with the four directions marked out and the inner shrines carefully placed so that the entire focus is gradually directed to the central image of the deity, which is the *bindu*, the point at the center. Thus the temple mirrors the cosmos.

Northern temples are most often characterized by a conical dome called a *shikara*. In earlier temples, only one *shikara* rose over the central image. Later the *shikara* grew to cover the entire temple, and then the temple was further elaborated to include areas in front of the shrine where worshipers could assemble. These could be covered by a flat roof or a second smaller *shikara*.

Brahma Says _____

A **shikara** is a conical dome over a northern temple. Many temples came to have multiple *shikaras* in ascending size, rising upwards like a mountain range.

Temples may also include an area set aside for traditional Vedic fire rituals. These rituals are only performed on rare occasions in modern times. Many of them had historically been sponsored by royalty and performed at special moments related to rulership, so as the monarchies disappeared, the rituals were no longer required. A few Brahmin families still preserve the ancient knowledge, and research foundations are trying to sponsor performances that can then be recorded on video so the ancient practices will not be completely lost. A renewed respect for the richness of tradition has also inspired efforts to sponsor performances of the old rituals more frequently.

Temple Images

Whether northern or southern in style, the heart of every temple is the *garbha-griha*, the "womb-house," where the central image of the deity resides. God is physically present within the *garbha-griha* in the form of the *murti*, the temple icon. Shiva temples usually have Shiva *lingams* as their central *murtis*, Vishnu temples have images of Vishnu or his *avataras* in human form, and Devi temples may have either nonrepresentational or representational forms.

> **Brahma Says** _____
>
> The **garbha-griha,** also called the "womb-house," is the inner sanctuary of a temple.

When devotees come to the temple, they come for *darshan*, "vision," in which they see the deity and are seen by the deity. The fact that the divine is present within the *murti* does not mean that God is limited to the image. The divine is infinite and can take on any number of forms without ever lessening itself. The physical image in the temple is a form provided for the benefit of the devotee.

Of course, some Hindus do not approve of *murti* worship. They argue that the divine is infinite and formless, so no physical object can be more than a symbolic representation. Shankara, the great Vedantin philosopher, mediated between these viewpoints by teaching that the worship of an image was a way to focus your devotion and prepare for the higher worship of the formless Absolute. It is notable, however, that even Vedantins tend to worship at shrines.

Temples have creation stories describing how the deities came to reside there. Many of the creation stories are linked to the epic and Puranic narratives. One of the most popular temples to Vishnu is at

Tirupati. Here the god is called Venkateshwara, the Lord of Venkata hill. According to tradition, this hill was brought to its present site at Vishnu's behest when the god decided to rest there after he had incarnated as a boar and rescued the earth from submersion in the universal waters.

Some temple stories tell how the god or goddess manifested at that location because of the devotion of a particular saint. A temple may be built because a king prayed and asked God to become permanently present in a specific location and the Lord chose to honor the request. Often, in a temple dedicated to Shiva, the narrative will recount how Shiva came to the area and married the local goddess. This is the case at the Minakshi temple in Madurai.

Bet You Didn't Know

Shiva came to Madurai to marry Minakshi, the queen of the Pandyan kingdom, and became her co-ruler as Sundareshwara. The marriage of the deities is celebrated annually at the temple. Certain shrines devoted to Devi are identified with the tale about the dismemberment of Sati recounted in Chapter 5.

Temples may also be built when a local deity needs a new home. In the Konku region of Tamil Nadu, the goddess Kali (known locally as Kaliyatta) visited

a family and demanded that a temple be built for
her. She had previously resided in a coconut grove,
where a *trishula* (trident) was the symbolic embodiment of her presence. But as the town grew, the
grove was replaced by housing and the goddess was
almost forgotten as her abode disappeared. The
establishment of a temple gave her a new home.

Temple Rituals

Rituals within the temples are performed by professional priests. The core ritual is *puja*, the worship
of the *murti*. In *puja*, the deity is treated as a royal
guest.

Hindu Hints

In *puja*, the deity is bathed, adorned
with clothing and garlands of flowers, and
offered food and drink. When special
portable images are carried in processions, the deities are shaded by umbrellas.
Music and dance performances are offered
for their entertainment. The priests make
offerings of fruit, flowers, or coconuts to the
deities.

The last part of the ritual is the *arati*, in which the
priests wave lighted lamps or camphor flames in
front of the *murtis*. During the *arati*, many devotees
raise their hands to their foreheads with the palms
pressed together in a gesture of salutation. The

priest then brings the camphor flame out to the crowd and people cup their hands over the flame then touch their eyes. Through this gesture the deity's power and protective grace are transmitted to the devotees.

Brahma Says _____

Arati is the waving of a flame or lamp during worship, during the last part of the *puja* ritual.

After the *puja*, the devotees receive *prasada*, which literally means "grace." The *prasada* may be some of the fruit or flowers that were offered to the *murti* or water and other liquids that were used in the ritual bathing of the deity. In Shiva temples the *prasada* is often white ash, a substance especially associated with that god. The food is eaten, the water may be sprinkled over the head and some of it swallowed, and the ash is usually smeared on the forehead although a little of it may also be swallowed. All of these substances have been in contact with the deity during the *puja* and have become imbued with divine power and grace that are then transferred to the devotee who receives them. *Prasada* is the culmination of the *puja* ritual.

Brahma Says _____

Prasada means the grace of God; ritual offerings given to devotees; it is the conclusion to the *puja* ritual.

The scene within a temple where this *puja* takes place is very different from the congregational service of a Christian church. The devotees do not engage in a single, synchronized group liturgy. Although they gather together to watch the priests make offerings, the temple experience is largely personal. It is as individuals that people approach the deity to offer prayers and receive *darshan*, to listen to the priest's recitations, make donations to the temple, and receive *prasada*. This does not mean that there is no social component to public rituals. There is constant activity in a temple. Not only are the priests performing rituals at least three times a day to each image, but there is a constant stream of people in and out of the area.

People prostrate themselves before the deity and offer prayers, while others sit quietly in meditation. Groups may come together to sing devotional songs. Sick folks sit in the temple patiently waiting for the gods to heal them. Children play games while adults sit in corners and read scriptures or chat with friends. The temple is a hive of activity. But the interaction between devotee and deity takes place on a personal level.

In general, *puja* is performed to please the gods. If the deities are properly honored, the community should prosper under divine protection, and conversely, if the deities are displeased, there may be trouble. Some priests say modern problems are the result of improper ritual performance. But they are quick to point out that, even if the rituals are perfectly carried out, the deity is not compelled to act in a particular way. Gods cannot be controlled by mortals.

Although ideally worship is performed out of love for God, in fact most people go to the temples to ask for boons from the gods. Deities are approached for community aid in times of drought, flood, famine, or epidemic. They are also petitioned for personal aid regarding such matters as sickness, fertility, and household finances. It is, however, frequently said that these daily issues are too insignificant for the great gods and such matters are more often taken to local divinities. This then falls into the category of domestic worship.

The Least You Need to Know

- By the classical period, temples had become the focus of rituals; instead of gods who resided in the atmosphere and were worshiped through the intermediary of the fire that carried offerings up to the heavens, the gods were now established in specific locations.

- Whether northern or southern in style, the heart of every temple is the *garbha-griha*, the "womb-house," where the central image of the deity resides.

- Rituals within the temples are performed by professional priests. The core ritual is *puja*, the worship of the *murti*. In *puja*, the deity is treated as a royal guest.

Domestic Worship

In This Chapter

- Household deities
- Renunciants, healers, and dancers
- Learning the life-cycle rituals

Hindu worship takes place in two spheres: the domain of the temple (previous chapter) and the domestic sphere. The timing of most religious practices within both of these realms is carefully regulated. On the individual level, rituals may be performed to mark transition points in a person's life or responses to family situations. On a more general level, rituals are performed at specific times of the day, month, and year as determined by the lunar-solar calendar that governs Hinduism.

Shrines to the Deities

Domestic worship has many of the same attributes as the temple tradition. Each home has an area set aside for the household deities, either in a special room or on a shelf within a room. The household altar usually has several images because the members of the family may worship different deities. People have an *ishtadevata*, a "chosen deity," with whom they have a special relationship.

A family may have Shiva as its tutelary deity, but one brother's wife may come from a family devoted to the goddess Durga and another brother may have become a devotee of Krishna. So, all three deities may be established on the family altar in the form of sculptures or pictures. Other deities with specific functions like Ganesha, the remover of obstacles, and Sarasvati, goddess of knowledge, may flank the main images. There may also be pictures of great saints.

Hindu Hints

Nonrepresentational images like the Shiva *lingam* and the *shalagrama* stone, which bears the imprint of a fossilized fish that represents Vishnu, are common in homes. The *shalagrama* is placed on a small silver casket shaped like the great serpent on which Vishnu sleeps in Puranic mythology.

Local gods and goddesses are often more prominent in domestic worship than Vishnu, Shiva, and Devi because many Hindus believe the latter are primarily concerned with the creation, preservation, and destruction of the cosmos, while regional deities care for the daily concerns of people. These gods and goddesses are usually specific to a locale. Most villages have a protective divinity, usually a goddess. There may also be specific deities linked to particular kinship groups. Because of their strong ties to the place and the people, these deities are actively concerned with the welfare of the community. They are petitioned for aid with weather and crops and are especially helpful with disease and fertility.

Some local goddesses have particular associations with diseases. Sitala, in the north, and Mariyamman, in the south, are goddesses of smallpox (now eradicated). These two deities have regional followings not limited to specific villages, but they are not pan-Hindu. The theory of ritual temperature plays a major role in explaining epidemics. Village goddesses who are associated with epidemic diseases can become overheated physically and emotionally. If they become too hot and emotional, their heated rage may manifest in feverish diseases. The people who are infected are considered possessed by the goddess and are said to help her by sharing the pent-up heat that has become too much for her to bear alone. The victims are worshiped with cooling rituals and animal sacrifices are performed to placate and cool the goddess.

In general, the types of offerings made to deities differ between Brahmin-run temples and village folk traditions. Gods and goddesses who live in large temples usually receive vegetarian offerings while the village deities may also require offerings of alcohol and blood sacrifices of chickens, goats, and sometimes buffalos. If a village deity gains a wider following and is adopted into a priestly temple tradition, substitutions like colored water instead of blood will be made for these non-vegetarian offerings. The distinction between vegetarian and non-vegetarian deities does have exceptions, especially in the case of the goddess who sometimes receives both kinds of offerings. During a festival, Devi may be represented in two forms, one a nonrepresentational image, such as a pot of water, and the other a bronze *murti*. Blood sacrifices will be made to the pot, while the bronze image receives only vegetarian offerings. In this way, the folk traditions and the priestly practices are carried out side by side.

On the Right Path

Local deities sometimes have small temples devoted to them, but more often they are worshiped in simple outdoor shrines. The *murtis* in these shrines are often nonrepresentational; perhaps a pot of water, a tree, a trident called a *trishula*, or a rock painted red. The shrine for the village goddess may stand on the boundaries of the community where she can protect her people from malevolent outside forces. Deified people are often worshiped at their tombs.

Major gods may become overheated and require human aid to maintain a thermal balance just like the local disease goddesses. In the hill temple at Palani, the Tamil god Murukan is worshiped as a healer. But the healing qualities of the god can be affected by seasonal and astral influences, as well as by the strain caused by attending to the pleas of countless devotees. Two festivals are held, one at the height of the cold season and one in the hot season, to help balance the god's temperature. In the hot season, pilgrims bring pots of water from the Kaveri River, which is said to be as cooling as water from the Ganges itself, for the bathing of the *murtis*. During the winter festival, pilgrims bring Murukan offerings of unrefined sugar, which is believed to be a heating substance.

Some local divinities are deified people, either heroes or placated ghosts. The heroes may be saints who led lives of devotion, warriors who died in defense of the community, or women who carried wifely *dharma* to its ultimate expression by becoming *sati*, that is by committing suicide on their husbands' funeral pyres. Such people attain divinity through the purity of their actions in life. They are then able to help those who honor them. Because of their human origins, such deities are considered to have special affinity for the concerns of the mortal world, especially the people who live in their former community. The ghosts, on the other hand, are worshiped in order to prevent them from causing harm. Malevolent ghosts are the spirits of people who meet bad deaths, such as murder, suicide, accident, disease, childbirth, or any event that causes premature death. The victim dies without fulfillment, and is therefore unhappy and likely to cause pain to the living who enjoy the things the deceased missed out on. So, for example, women who die childless may become spirits that are dangerous to infants. By enshrining and worshiping the ghost, the malevolent spirit can be controlled and even made beneficial. Usually family members of the deceased perform such worship, but if the deified ghost gains a reputation for being able to help people, it may gain a wider following.

Religious Specialists

Besides the Brahmin priests, there are numerous other religious specialists who play roles in domestic religious experiences. Among these are renunciants, folk healers, exorcists, and mediums that deities possess.

Renunciants

Renunciants, called *sadhus*, come in diverse guises. Some belong to monastic organizations, like those founded by Shankara, and others are solitary hermits. Some wear orange robes and others go naked as part of their discipline to break free of all bonds. Some engage in rigorous ascetic practices, others follow the path of *jnana-yoga*, combining meditation with study and contemplation of scripture.

Despite their different paths, *sadhus* are revered as holy people, for they have left the security of worldly life and devoted themselves entirely to religious seeking. Such *sadhus* may pass through a community while on pilgrimage or settle near a town to

pursue their ascetic practices. The community sup-
ports these ascetics through food offerings and
gifts. Occasionally the ascetic will give advice or
religious teachings to those who seek his counsel.
Because *sadhus* practice yoga, they are believed to
have extraordinary powers. Consequently people
may ask for their aid in overcoming local problems
like drought.

People may also go to gurus for advice. Gurus are
religious teachers who work closely with a small
number of disciples, but they also interact with a
wider community of people who revere them for
their spiritual attainment and their special ability to
help others on the religious path. Some gurus are
sadhus, but others are householders. Householder
gurus may have turned their attention from material to devote themselves to spiritual pursuits but
have not found it necessary to take vows of renunciation. Often family members are among their disciples, and the position of spiritual leader may be
passed on to a descendant.

Healers

Alongside these overtly religious figures, there are
people like healers whose work depends on knowledge of the relation between the physical body,
spirits, and the workings of the cosmos. Healers
apply ancient systems of medicine based on the
idea that illness is the result of imbalances in the
body caused by such things as improper diet, excessive exertion, evil spirits, and exposure to heat or
cold. Medicine, rituals, and changes in diet are
prescribed to cure illness.

Possession is widespread in rural Hinduism, especially in south India. There are different types of possession. In unwanted possessions, ghosts or demons take control of a person and must be exorcised by a professional exorcist. There are also formalized ritual institutions of possession. Among these are professional fortunetellers who act as mediums and a pattern of possession in relation to the fulfillment of vows. People seeking divine aid promise to honor a deity by taking part in a pilgrimage or a procession, and during the procession the god or goddess often possesses them.

"Dancers"

There are also specialists who become possessed by a deity on a regular basis in the context of specific rituals. One example is the *camiyati*, the "god dancer" of south India. The *camiyati* becomes possessed and serves as a temporary mouthpiece for a deity during festivals.

Bet You Didn't Know

The dancers are known for ascetic feats, such as walking on hot coals, which serve as proof of their possessed state and attest to the power of the deity who protects them from pain and harm. While the god dancer is possessed, people can ask for advice and reassurance.

Often the various roles of healer, counselor, and soothsayer are blended together since they are attributes of divinity and the possessed person is assimilated to a deity. This is evident in the case of Valliyamma, a south Indian woman who was called to serve Murukan.

Valliyamma was born into a family that was devoted to Murukan. Every year they made a pilgrimage to the Palani hill temple. When Valliyamma was 12 years old, she became possessed by the god during this pilgrimage. He instructed her to fast and keep silent for six months. After completing this period, she had a dream in which Murukan told her to walk for seven days around the neighboring villages with a needle pierced through her tongue and then return to the Palani temple.

During this tour, the girl became possessed by the god and danced along the streets of the villages, so people began to call her a *camiyati*, a god dancer. When she reached the temple, the god again possessed her and gave her a secret mantra that enabled her to cure diseases and predict the future. Since then, devotees have come to her for healing and advice. She performs *pujas* to a framed picture of Murukan in her room, which has become a "temple-house" and distributes sacred ashes and water to devotees after the ritual, just like a temple priest.

Samskaras—Life-Cycle Rituals

The *samskaras*, often called the sacraments of Hinduism, are rites that guide the Hindu along the path of *dharma*, of virtuous living. The word *samskara* means "perfecting." These ceremonies combine the elements of *puja*, prayer, utterance of ancient hymns, and communal feasting. Birth, initiation, marriage, and death are the most frequently observed rites. There are also numerous regional rituals performed by women to celebrate puberty, acquire good husbands, secure the welfare of their families, and encourage each other during pregnancy.

Birth

The ceremonies that surround the birth of a child include sponsoring *pujas* at the local temple and reciting prayers of petition for a long life attended by good fortune. It is important to note the exact moment of birth so that a horoscope can be cast for the child. The horoscope will be especially important for arranging a suitable marriage when the child grows up. Special celebrations may also be held to mark a child's naming, eating of first solid food, and first haircut. Children are supposed to receive auspicious names so they are often named after deities and heroes.

Upanayana

The initiation ritual, called *upanayana*, marks a child's entry into the student stage of life. A boy is ritually bathed and dressed in special garments and brought to a teacher of the ancient Vedic lore. The teacher invests the lad with a sacred thread, a triple strand of three threads to be worn over the left shoulder, and gives him his first lesson in the Vedas.

Brahma Says

Upanayana is an initiation or a sacred-thread ceremony. It was originally held for boys of the three higher castes, but today is common only with the Brahmins.

This first lesson is memorization of the Gayatri mantra, "I meditate on the brilliance of the sun; may it illumine my mind," which the boy should recite daily for the rest of his life. In past days, the young initiate would go to live with a teacher and study, but now the ritual mostly has a social function. After the ceremony, there is a feast and the boy receives gifts.

Women's Puberty Rituals

Women's rites are not part of the Sanskrit textual tradition, but they are part of all the regional cultures of South Asia. Celebration of a girl's first period is found in most rural communities, although the traditions are no longer observed much in urban areas. Among the Aiyar women of Tamil Nadu, the girl stays in a darkened room for three days. On the fourth day, she purifies herself with a ritual bath and there is a feast. Her mother takes her to the temple and then to visit other households where older women wave *arati* (flame or lamp during worship) lights to her.

In other areas, the family celebrates by dressing their daughter in new clothes, adorning her hair with flowers, and feeding her special foods. The festivities may take the form of a miniature wedding, in which the girl's family gives her money or clothing.

Marriage

Marriage is the biggest life-cycle ritual in most people's lives. When two people marry, they enter the householder stage of life, in which they fulfill their duties to family and society. Marriage is a great transition into responsibility.

Marriage rites differ from region to region. First the parents must arrange a suitable match. They draw on their extended kin networks to find prospective spouses and may also consult classified ads in newspapers where they find information about available parties in more distant areas, even in other countries.

Ideally the bride and groom will come from the same area, speak the same language, and be from the same caste. Responsible parents try to find their children partners of similar educational background and good temperament. A girl's family will also take into consideration a groom's potential earning ability to ensure her future security and make sure that he does not have too many younger siblings since his wife may end up working too hard to serve them.

Bet You Didn't Know

The horoscopes of the bride and groom must be compatible. In the modern technological age, computers often match horoscopes. Not only must the astrological signs be complementary, but it is believed that each person's life has periods of good and bad fortune. The ups and downs predicted for two people should line up so as to counterbalance each other to prevent excessive hardship.

Once an appropriate match is found, the families meet as a group and later the bride and groom will have a chance to meet, too. Sometimes the couple insists on having time to get to know each other before committing to a wedding. Today, urban life and coeducational schooling has increased the number of "love matches," but arranged marriages are still quite common.

The actual marriage ritual involves prayers, walking around a fire altar, and the utterance of auspicious mantras by a priest. The wedding prayers ask for strength in adversity, health, children, long life, and faith in each other. A good life has these ingredients. Through marriage, the bride and groom become partners in household *dharma*. Together they fulfill their obligations to the family ancestors by having children (sons) to ensure that the ancestral rites will continue, and they fulfill their duties to the gods by performing domestic rites in their home.

Marriage is also a great social celebration with processions, exchanges of gifts, and feasting. Guests are entertained with music, dance, and fireworks. Weddings are an expression of social status and families spend as much as they can, even going into debt to put on an elaborate show. Sometimes the festivities last for several days even though the actual wedding ritual only requires a few hours.

Death

At death, the family prepares the body of the deceased, carries it in a procession to the cremation grounds, and recites specific prayers while the body is cremated. The god of death is called upon to give the deceased a good place among the ancestors, and other deities are also invoked to intercede on behalf of the departed loved one. The god of fire is asked to carry the dead person safely to the realm of ancestors. Once cremated, the ashes and bones of the deceased are either committed to a holy river or buried. *Sadhus* and small children are usually buried without cremation.

After the funeral, the family members go to a brook or river to purify themselves with ritual baths. Because of death, the family will be in a state of ritual impurity for a prescribed amount of time and will have to limit interaction with others. The spirit of the dead person is a ghost for the first few days and must be fed in a ritual called *shraddha* until it moves on to the realm of the ancestors. This rite centers on offerings of nourishment and prayers for the welfare of deceased relatives.

The eldest son offers the ghost water and balls of rice to cool the spirit after the cremation and give it strength for its journey. Once the spirit moves on to the next world, the eldest son must continue to perform the *shraddha* rite for his ancestors on the new moon day of each month for the first year after the death of his parents. After a year passes, the rite is performed annually. Because *shraddha* is the duty of the son, Hindus set great importance on the birth of a male child. Without a son to perform the *shraddha* rites, the deceased would be stuck as a ghost forever.

The Least You Need to Know

- In domestic worship, each home has an area set aside for the household deities, either in a special room or on a shelf within a room.

- Numerous religious specialists (aside from Brahmin priests) play roles in domestic religious experiences: renunciants, folk healers, exorcists, and mediums who are possessed by deities.

- The *samskaras*, often called the sacraments of Hinduism, are rites that guide the Hindu along the path of *dharma*, of virtuous living.

- The life-cycle rituals are ceremonies that combine the elements of *puja*, prayer, utterance of ancient hymns, and communal feasting; birth, initiation, marriage, and death are the most frequently observed rites.

Chapter 9

Revival and Reform

In This Chapter

- The Hindu religious tradition defined
- The first reform movement: Brahmo Samaj
- The second reform movement: Arya Samaj
- Saint Ramakrishna and his disciple Vivekananda

The beliefs and practices described in the preceding chapters still pervade Hindu life in the modern world, but new developments in the nineteenth and twentieth centuries have caused some changes in Hinduism. The nineteenth century brought revival and reform movements within Hinduism and a new effort to define Hindu *dharma* in relation to other world religions. This need for definition continued into the twentieth century when it became part of the formation of Indian nationalism.

Today, defining Hinduism is closely tied to issues of Indian identity, both within the boundaries of the subcontinent and in other countries all around the world. Modern Hindu *dharma* is also being reshaped by the necessity of adapting to new social settings in this era of urbanization and global migration.

Hindus Define Their Religious Tradition

The nineteenth century brought an era of revival and reform in Hindu religious life. During this period, Hindus consciously set out to define their religious tradition. Definition is most necessary in order to distinguish one tradition from another, and throughout the history of South Asia, religions such as Buddhism and Islam had distinguished themselves as other than the brahmanical tradition, so previously it had not been the mainstream that needed defining.

In the nineteenth century, under British rule, some Hindus began to feel the need to consciously define their tradition. They were influenced by numerous factors such as pressures from Christian missionaries, the experience of traveling to England and being in a land where none of the foundations of their cultural system were present, and being educated in British schools.

The Western education brought with it an assumption of a distinction between religion and social practices, which, in turn, made it possible to critique "social" practices that were not considered acceptable, even if they had been imbued with authority through religious institutions. This set the stage for religious reform, but the leaders of these reforms did not wish to throw out Hinduism and replace it with Western traditions, only to eliminate practices deemed unworthy of a great world religion.

On the Right Path

The leaders of the reform movements had tremendous pride in the religious heritage of Hinduism, especially in the sophisticated philosophy of the Vedas and the Upanishads. Thus reform was accompanied by a revival of interest in the ancient texts.

Brahmo Samaj

The first reform movement was the Brahmo Samaj, founded in 1828 by Ram Mohan Roy (1772–1833). Roy came from a Bengali Brahmin family, was educated at a Muslim university, and worked for the British East India Company in Calcutta. In the course of his studies, he explored both Eastern and Western philosophy. In his reform movement, he drew on ideas from the Upanishads, Shankara's *Advaita Vedanta*, Islamic Sufi theology, Unitarianism, and Deism.

He believed in a Deistic-style God, a transcendent creator who cannot be known because its essence is ineffable. He thought all religions had this same conception at their centers, despite the differences in their external practices, so he advocated tolerance and the belief that all religions are essentially one. Roy focused on reason and ethics. Through reason and the observation of the divinely created natural world, one could know God and perceive universal moral laws.

Roy considered the teachings of the Upanishads and the *Brahma Sutras* to be the highest wisdom and wanted to purify Hinduism by eliminating ethical degenerations that had accrued to the tradition in later centuries. He campaigned against practices such as child-marriage and *sati*, neither of which had a basis in the religion of the Upanishads.

Bet You Didn't Know

Ram Mohan Roy deplored Puranic and Tantric ritual practices, especially image worship. In fact, he had little sympathy for popular religion and accepted only the Upanishadic conception of the divine as an impersonal Absolute.

The practices of the Brahmo Samaj were modeled on Christian services. The meetings included readings from the Upanishads, sermons, and hymns. Roy also worked to establish Western scientific education in India. Some time after Roy's death, a schism occurred between members who stopped wearing their sacred threads in order to show their belief that there was no inequality between lower and higher castes and more conservative members who believed in caste hierarchy.

This schism and the issues that concerned the group reflect the place of the members within the social order. Child-marriage and *sati* were essentially high-caste practices prior to the twentieth century. The rejection of popular theism in favor of belief in an impersonal Brahman is the position of an educated elite, not the average villager for whom personal devotion is the most important part of religious experience. The Brahmo Samaj appealed to Brahmins who were not highly orthodox and to the newly emerging, urban middle class. The membership was not large, but the movement set a precedent by making a distinction between social practices and religion and then calling for reform of social practices in terms of "correct" religious ethics. This critique challenged the definition of Hindu orthodoxy.

Arya Samaj

A second reform movement called the Arya Samaj was established in 1875 by Dayananda Sarasvati (1824–1883). Unlike the Brahmo Samaj, which accepted the superiority of Western science and some Western social ethics, the Arya Samaj believed that the Vedas were the highest source of knowledge and ethics in the world. Even later Sanskrit texts were of less value, the true revelation was in the hymns of the *Rig Veda*. The Arya Samaj inspired pride in the ancient heritage of Hinduism and actively opposed the missionary efforts of Christians and Muslims.

Based on the early Vedic hymns, the Arya Samaj advocated worship of an impersonal God and rejection of "superstitious" practices such as image worship, belief in incarnations, belief in the myths of the epics and Puranas, and Puranic practices like pilgrimage. None of these were part of the pure teachings in the Vedas. Dayananda actively worked for social reforms such as eliminating child-marriage to reduce the number of widows, allowing marriage by choice rather than arrangement, and encouraging education for both boys and girls. He believed education was the means to teach people to be good Hindus and to promote national unity. To further these educational goals, the Arya Samaj established schools called *gurukulas* throughout India. The schools teach Sanskrit, the linguistic symbol of India's heritage, and Hindi, which Dayananda promoted as a national language.

The emphasis on Hindi demonstrates the regional ties of the Arya Samaj. It has been most successful in northern India, where it has even succeeded in reconverting people from Christianity and Islam. The celebration of the Vedic heritage fosters pride in Indian identity and the movement had great appeal to the nineteenth-century merchant class and to Hindus settled in South Africa and Fiji. But, as with the Brahmo Samaj, there was little response from the masses for whom religious life meant devotion and a personal experience of the divine. In spite of the limited membership, however, the movement has been influential in establishing a link between Hinduism and national identity that has carried over into modern politics.

Ramakrishna Mission

Both the Arya Samaj and the Brahmo Samaj
were social reform movements that came out of a
Western-educated upper class. A separate influence
came from the Bengali devotional tradition through
the experiences of the saint Ramakrishna and his
disciple Vivekananda.

Ramakrishna (1836–1886) was born into a Vaishnava
Brahmin family and served as priest in a temple devoted to the goddess Kali, near Calcutta. He spent
his time in devotional practices like meditation and
singing hymns to the goddess and began to pass into trance-like states during which he had visions of
Kali. Finally, his absorption in devotion made it
necessary to appoint another priest to carry out the
temple activities.

Ramakrishna continued to live on the temple
grounds and made progress on his spiritual path
through the guidance of two gurus. The first was a
Brahmin woman who taught him Tantric practices
of discipline to control emotions and channel the
energies in his body. The second teacher was a *sadhu*
who instructed him in meditation techniques to
experience the identity between the self and
Brahman.

Ramakrishna had visions of many deities, including
Jesus Christ. He studied both Christianity and
Islam, and followed their teachings until he felt he
had reached the final goal of each tradition. In his
experience, the end of each path was the same so he

decided that all religions are true, they just take different paths to reach the same ultimate goal.

Ramakrishna was recognized as a saint during his life and had many followers. Among these was Narendranath Datta, a young member of the Brahmo Samaj, who became a *sannyasin* after meeting Ramakrishna and took the name Vivekananda. Swami Vivekananda (1863–1902) had a tremendous impact on the development of modern Hindu identity both in South Asia and in the West. He came to the United States in 1893, to take part in the World Parliament of Religions in Chicago, and the description of Hinduism he set forth in that forum became the basis for most Western interpretations of the tradition for much of the next century.

Bet You Didn't Know

Vivekananda struck a chord with his Western audience and became an instant celebrity in the United States. People were so interested in his teachings that he established the Vedanta Society in New York in 1895 to share his ideas with Americans. The acclaim Vivekananda received brought him world fame and made him a national hero back in India. His success inspired great pride among Hindus who, for the fist time, found that Westerners were publicly applauding their faith instead of telling them that it was a backward tradition that should be given up in favor of the more "modern" Christian religion.

Through Vivekananda's efforts, Hinduism gained respect as a world religion, on the same footing as Judaism, Christianity, Islam, and Buddhism.

Vivekananda's philosophy was based on Advaita Vedanta. He believed that the divine is all pervasive and the goal of life should be to realize one's identity with that divinity. Out of this life goal, Vivekananda developed social programs. Since the divine exists in all, there can be no higher or lower status. The effort to see the divine in oneself and others leads to compassion for all people. Established in 1897, the Ramakrishna Mission aids people through education, social reform, and healing the sick.

The Mission is guided by an order of monks who run its colleges, high schools, and hospitals. At the time of its organization, this monastic order was unique in India because its members gave their lives of service to the world rather than in ascetic isolation. The order teaches Vivekananda's "Neo-Vedanta" Hinduism, which stresses the idea of Hindu tolerance. All the sects within Hinduism and, indeed, all other religions are different paths to the same goal. This view has been criticized for oversimplifying Hindu traditions, but it has great appeal to the English-educated urban class who need a way to balance their traditional heritage with the modern world in which they must live.

The impulse toward religious reform was not new in the nineteenth century. Many of the great poet-saints had also criticized caste distinctions, the denigration of women, and empty ritualism. But these poets were leveling their complaints at problems within the sphere of religious life. They were trying to point out that caste and gender were not factors in determining one's relation to God, and that true devotion had greater value than priestly ritual. The poets were not trying to reform the social order beyond the realm of devotional practices.

In the nineteenth century, reformers began to criticize social practices that no longer seemed acceptable, even if they were popularly considered to have religious sanction. These challenges to tradition were bolstered by a revival of interest in the revelations contained in the Vedas and Upanishads.

The ancient texts became a source of "pure" religion and ethics, which were used to condemn social practices that did not have scriptural sanction and were not considered congruous with Vedic ideals. Gradually the medieval poet-saints came to be seen as forerunners of the nineteenth- and twentieth-century reformers, and their criticisms of religious institutions were extended to the larger social order. Today, most Hindus think of saints like Kabir, who challenged traditions, as social reformers.

The Least You Need to Know

- The nineteenth century brought an era of revival and reform in Hindu religious life. During this period, Hindus consciously set out to define their religious tradition.

- The practices of the Brahmo Samaj were modeled on Christian services. The meetings included readings from the Upanishads, sermons, and hymns.

- Based on the early Vedic hymns, the Arya Samaj advocated worship of an impersonal God and rejection of "superstitious" practices such as image worship, belief in incarnations, belief in the myths of the epics and Puranas, and Puranic practices like pilgrimage.

- The Ramakrishna Mission was a social influence (separate from the Brahmo Samaj and the Arya Samaj) that came from the Bengali devotional tradition through the experiences of the saint Ramakrishna and his disciple Vivekananda.

10

Hinduism: Nationalism and Globalism

In This Chapter

- Independence from British rule
- The connection between religious and national identity
- From traditions to new settings

Hinduism played a vital role in the development of Indian nationalism. Nationalism requires a central administration and a sense of shared identity as a body that supersedes personal and local identity. The British rule of India provided the centralized administration necessary for modern nationalism, but the ideology that drew the populace together was based on the shared idiom of Hinduism.

Despite different languages and cultures, and despite disparate deities and sects, Hinduism provided symbols and ideals that held appeal across the diverse regions and social classes of the subcontinent. This connection between Indian identity and Hindu identity has persisted in post-independence India, where it plays a role in politics and social movements.

The Independence Movement

Leaders of the movement for India's independence from British rule used Hindu practices and ideals to muster support from the populace. They stressed the otherness of the English as followers of a foreign faith and characterized government laws that affected long-established traditions as attacks on the Hindu religion. So, for example, when the government outlawed *sati* and decreed that widows could legally remarry, many Indians saw the new laws as part of a Christian conspiracy to subvert Hinduism even though members of the Brahmo Samaj and Arya Samaj had lobbied for these very reforms (see Chapter 9). The perceptions of foreign religious persecution helped create a sense of unity among Hindu Indians.

B. G. Talik (1856–1920) used Hinduism as a source of popular appeal in his efforts to unite people into nationalist groups, particularly in his home region of Maharashtra. Through journalism in Marathi, the regional language, he voiced opposition to British bills that challenged cultural traditions. He used traditional religious festivals as occasions for patriotic speeches and political education of the masses. He revived the Ganesha festival as a way to tap a specifically Hindu nationalism. He supported Cow

Protection Societies, which had a universal appeal in India.

> ### Hindu Hints
>
> For many people, the cow is a symbol of Hinduism. As a representation of fertility and the bounty of nature, the cow is a mother-symbol revered across sectarian boundaries. The Hindu ideal of not killing (*ahimsa*) is most widely applied to the belief that one should not harm cows, so the concern with protecting the cow from her enemies, the beef-eating British and Muslims, was a powerful unifier.

Tilak also drew on the legend of Shivaji, the great Maharashtrian chieftain who fought successfully against the Mughals in the seventeenth century. Just as Shivaji had driven out the Mughals, so too would the British be driven out. Tilak established a festival in honor of Shivaji's birth to promote the ideal of *svaraj*, "self-rule." Tilak himself was seen as a reincarnation of Shivaji, and some people even considered him an *avatara* of Vishnu, come, like Rama or Krishna, to restore the balance of righteousness.

One of the side effects of using allegories of Hindu heroes from the past was creating a nationalism that was implicitly anti-Muslim as well as anti-British. A similar pattern emerged in the Bengali literary movements of the same era. The Bengali literature was pervaded by a mystical nationalism that emphasized India's past, especially the deeds of the Rajput warriors who fought against the Muslim invaders. The Muslims in these works were symbolic of all foreign rulers and were essentially stand-ins for the British, but, over time, all Muslims became demonized.

A second theme in the Bengali literature was the image of India as a sacred land, personified as a goddess. The ideal of selfless devotion to Kali was transferred to Mother India, Bharat Mata. Mother India was a unifying symbol, the maternal deity of all her Hindu children. But here, too, there was no room for other religions; the sacred land was a Hindu goddess. Mohandas K. Gandhi (1869–1948) tried to include other religions, especially Islam, in his vision of independent India, but he also used the language of Hinduism to spread his nationalist message.

Gandhi emerged as a leader who combined the traditional life of a religious saint with the aspirations of a people seeking freedom from foreign rule. His great triumph was to bring the populace into the independence movement. He gave the people a sense of involvement in their nation's destiny and made individual identity part of national identity. His authority came from his status as a *sadhu*, a holy man, living in accord with Hindu *dharma*.

Yoga is believed to confer power over the body, mind, and the cosmos itself. As a *yogin*, following traditional practices of meditation, fasting, silence, celibacy, and non-injury to other beings, Gandhi had the power and authority of a religious teacher, and he became the guru of the masses. He also used religious models in his campaign for independence. He went on pilgrimages to educate people and protest laws. He advocated nonviolent protest in accord with the Hindu belief in avoiding causing harm to other beings (*ahimsa*). He described the goal of independence as establishment of Ram Rajya, "the Kingdom of Rama," the rule of dharmic order associated with Lord Rama in the *Ramayana*. Gandhi also connected Hinduism with social work through the ideal of *sarvodaya*, "the uplift of all." He extended the traditional idea of *dharma* as duty to one's family and community to include duty toward the nation of India and all her citizens.

In 1947, the subcontinent achieved independence, but not as one nation. It was partitioned to create a separate Muslim country of Pakistan in the two regions with majority Muslim populations. Later eastern Pakistan became Bangladesh. The partition caused millions of Hindus and Muslims to migrate from their homes and the process was accompanied by terrible bloodshed. The loss of life, of family lands, and of livelihoods created bitterness on both sides of the border. In subsequent years, there have been periodic bouts of violence between the two religious communities as the sense of separate identities based on religion continues to grow stronger.

The tension between Hindus and Muslims is only the most blatant example of a situation called *communalism.* This division along religious lines can also be a division along sectarian lines. Members of a group share a common idiom, and it is always easy to see those who do not belong as the "other." From the early twentieth century, the practice of granting special privileges and representation in government to minority groups has contributed to this divisiveness. Furthermore, the weak are encouraged to stay weak in order to retain their privileges. This perpetuates class divisions and teaches people to think in terms of partisan groups, not as a nation.

> **Brahma Says** _____
>
> **Communalism** means the defining of social and political interests through primary reference to religious communities.

Hindutva = Hinduness

The constitution of India defines the nation as a secular state, but grants protective privileges to various minority groups so they will have representation and opportunities in spite of their limited numbers. Some of these groups are minority religions, like Islam, Christianity, Sikhism, and Jainism. Others are lower caste communities that have traditionally been at the bottom of the social hierarchy. So, for example, the government reserves a certain portion of civil service jobs for the untouchable castes, which are now called Dalits ("oppressed").

This system of reserving jobs and political representation for minority groups has created conflicts. Many Hindus feel that, as the majority, they should be able to have a state organized in accord with their beliefs and the minorities, as small groups within the state, should not be given preferential treatment. The conflict is further exacerbated by a shortage of jobs for both skilled and unskilled workers. Several organizations have emerged over the years to promote the rights of the Hindu majority and to advocate the creation of a Hindu state.

Hindu Mahasabha

One of the earliest such organizations was the Hindu Mahasabha, formed in 1906 to safeguard the Hindu way of life. Its members saw political efforts to placate minorities as contrary to the interests of Hindus. The adoption of Western secular ideas and the "excessive" concessions to the Muslims made to preserve unity during the struggle for independence were seen as betrayals of Hindu heritage. The organization was revived in the 1920s.

At that time V. D. Savarkar, one of its leaders, coined the term Hindutva to explain the connection between religious and national identity. Hindutva means "Hinduness." For Savarkar, a Hindu is one whose ancestors lived in India and who regards India as a holy land and the cradle of religion. In this definition he described a cultural Hinduism shared by the people of India. This identity is extended to Sikhs, Buddhists, and Jains because their religions developed in India, but excludes Christianity and Islam.

> **Bet You Didn't Know**
>
> The VHP is not a purely conservative movement. Although it sets forward the ideal of a Hindu society, it also maintains that the age-old dharmic code of conduct must be rearranged to meet the needs of changed times. The application of this principle is evident in the efforts to include the backward or untouchable castes. Where once such people were not allowed inside temples, now the VHP actively encourages them to take part in Hindu rituals.

Vishva Hindu Parishad (VHP)

The Vishva Hindu Parishad (VHP), which was founded in 1964, is the most influential organization working to promote the ideal of a Hindu state. The VHP brings together religious leaders from a wide range of sects and includes representatives from outside India. It works to revitalize Hindu dharma all over the world. According to the VHP, the term "Hindu" refers to "all people who believe in, respect or follow the eternal values of life—ethical and spiritual—that have evolved in Bharat [India]." The organization works to strengthen the Hindu community by unifying it. Unification is accomplished by renovating temples, building schools, promoting the study of Sanskrit, protecting cows, working to uplift the backward castes, and actively combating conversion to other religions.

In the 1980s and 1990s, the VHP's popularity grew. In the realm of politics, the exponential increase in electoral support for members of the Bharatiya Janata Party (BJP), which uses the Hindu nationalist ideology of the VHP, shows its widespread appeal. This increase in support, and the subsequent utilization of VHP ideals in politics, grew out of remarkably effective campaign strategies. One of these strategies was the Sacrifice for Unity procession held in 1983. This actually involved three large processions, fed by numerous smaller, tributary cavalcades, crossing the entire subcontinent. Their meeting point at Nagpur was compared to the confluence of the three sacred rivers at Allahabad.

Hindu Hints

Bharat Mata is equated with all the local goddesses worshiped in India, and indeed as the embodiment of the land itself she contains all holy sites within herself. Similarly all the sacred water in India is ultimately derived from the Ganges. So both Mother India and the Ganges water are symbols of Hindu unity. This unity was extended beyond the boundaries of the subcontinent by international participation in the Sacrifice for Unity.

The processions followed the format of a temple festival; each included a chariot (in this case a truck rather than a cart that needed to be carried or pulled) carrying an image of Bharat Mata, a large pot filled with water from the Ganges River, and a smaller pot containing local holy water.

A small procession from Bhutan traveled into India to join up with one of the main groups. A delegation from Burma brought water from their holy river, and others brought sacred water from Mauritius, Pakistan, and Bangladesh.

The VHP tries to create a modern Hinduism as the national religion of India. Unity is seen as a source of strength to help Hindus resist outside forces that threaten them through conversions to foreign religions and internal problems caused by conflicts among Hindus. Opposition to foreign traditions— Christianity and Islam—has been one of the themes of the organization. This theme played a major role when Hindus destroyed a Muslim mosque, called the Babri Masjid, in Ayodhya in December 1992.

The Babri Masjid was built in 1528 by a follower of the Mughal ruler, Babur. According to tradition, the mosque was built on the site of an older Hindu temple that commemorated the birthplace of Rama, the hero of the *Ramayana*. Prior to independence, Muslims worshiped inside the mosque and Hindus worshiped outside the building. In 1947, the Indian government closed the building to both communities. Then, in 1949, an image of Rama was placed in the mosque during the night and a rumor spread that the deity had appeared to reclaim his temple. Police quelled the riots that ensued, and the mosque remained closed.

In 1984, the Vishva Hindu Parishad took up the issue of reclaiming the temple site as part of their nationalist movement. They took images of Rama and Sita on a procession to Ayodhya, and then on to the capital, Delhi, holding rallies and making speeches. Over the next few years, the temple/mosque issue was taken up in the platforms of political parties and it became a central issue for the Bharatiya Janata Party. The story of Lord Rama has particular resonance as a political ideal. Rama was the divine king, the lord of *dharma*, who ruled over a golden age. Gandhi himself had evoked the image of Ram Rajya, the "rule of Rama," as the ideal society. A political party that could ally itself with the image of Lord Rama and his virtuous reign had a powerful pan-Indian appeal.

The power of the image of Rama was clear in 1987 to 1988, when the *Ramayana* television series aired and millions of people in India and in other countries tuned in to watch it every Sunday. The popularity of the series may have inspired politicians to renew their emphasis on the image of Rama and his kingdom in Ayodhya. In 1989, the VHP organized processions to bring bricks to Ayodhya to build a new temple on Rama's birthplace. These bricks came from villages all over India and from supporters in the United States, Canada, the Caribbean, and South Africa. Authorities did not allow the marchers to dismantle the Babri Masjid but some of the bricks were used to lay a foundation in a pit outside the mosque.

The effort to remove the mosque gained strength in 1990, after two political developments. First, the ongoing dispute between Pakistan and India over control of the region of Kashmir caused a new rash of violence. Second, the Indian government tried to increase the number of places reserved for backward castes in educational institutions and the civil service. The VHP started another ritual procession to Ayodhya with the goal of building a new temple in order to counteract the disunity caused by the anti-reservation riots.

During this procession, L. K. Advani, the leader of the BJP, posed as Lord Rama. The national government took a stand in support of the secularism of the nation, and the procession was not allowed to reach the mosque. As a result, the BJP withdrew its support of the government in parliament, and the leaders who had resisted the movement lost power. The publicity from the Ayodhya marches contributed to BJP success in elections, and in 1991, they gained control of the state government in Uttar Pradesh. In 1992, the VHP and BJP organized a rally in Ayodhya, and the mosque was destroyed.

The national government condemned the destruction. President's rule was imposed on Uttar Pradesh and BJP governments in three other states were dismissed. Hindu organizations like the VHP, which had been so instrumental in the Ayodhya campaign, were banned. Moreover, the government said it would rebuild the mosque. But the trouble was not limited to Ayodhya. Communal violence broke out in major cities like Calcutta and Mumbai (Bombay), where most of the fatalities were Muslims. There were answering riots in Pakistan and Bangladesh as Muslims attacked Indian businesses and Hindu temples. In Britain, Hindu temples and cultural centers, a Muslim mosque, and a Sikh *gurudwara* were fire-bombed. Black Muslims protested outside the United Nations in New York.

The destruction of the mosque and the international echoes of that action show how powerful the connection between religion and national identity has become. But the aftermath also shows that the beliefs that brought some people to commit violence are not universal. Most Hindus deplore the destruction and bloodshed. They recall Gandhi's campaign of nonviolence as a higher ideal, and a true mark of the greatness of Hinduism. Reaction to the violence following the destruction of the Babri Masjid seems to have blunted the appeal of political campaigns based on communalism. Politicians relying on "us versus them" rhetoric have lost ground in elections since 1992.

The Global Span of Modern Hinduism

The echoes of the Ayodhya conflict in London and New York demonstrate the global span of modern

Hinduism. During the nineteenth and twentieth centuries, Hindus spread out from their homeland so that they now live all around the world. The experiences of those who live in the "diaspora" has affected the way they define Hinduism.

Traditions that were taken for granted when they were part of the mainstream have taken on new meanings and have been adapted to new settings. At the same time, the adaptations and evaluations made abroad filter back to South Asia where they influence developments in Mother India.

Hindu Emigration Waves

There have been two waves of Hindu emigration in the modern period. The first occurred during the nineteenth and early twentieth centuries. In the nineteenth century, the quest for work caused Indians to emigrate to Burma (Myanmar), Sri Lanka, Malaysia, South Africa, the Fiji Islands, and the West Indies. By the 1920s, there were approximately two million Indians living abroad, mostly in British colonies and dominions. Most of these emigrants were indentured laborers.

In spite of discrimination, lack of educational facilities, and high mortality rates, they prospered in their new environments. They typically lived in ethnic communities where they could follow the traditions of their homeland. Temples were established, and priests (not necessarily Brahmins) were employed to perform traditional rituals. The practices included the full range of folk traditions.

The second wave, which really gained momentum in the 1960s and continues to this day, is made up of middle-class, educated urbanites. These city folks are migrating to the urban centers of the United States, Great Britain, Canada, and the economic centers of Asia like Singapore. They are professionals, doctors, engineers, and computer programmers, seeking economic opportunities because there are not enough jobs in India for all her college graduates.

Unlike the refugee immigrants of Eastern Europe and Southeast Asia, these middle-class Hindus do not settle in ethnic ghettoes. They move into suburban areas where there are good schools for their children. Most of these immigrants quickly gain middle-class status in their new countries, because they are well educated and speak English. The East Indians who live in the United States have become known as the most successful immigrant community in the history of the nation.

During the first years in their new land, the immigrants were focused on economic success and did not worry about the lack of facilities for religious life. They did, however, feel a need for cultural identity and numerous "cultural centers" were established where Indians could gather together. A great sense of shared Indian identity transcended all regional cultural divisions among the immigrants in the 1960s. If a cultural center showed a Bengali film, even those who could not understand the language were delighted to have the opportunity to watch something "Indian."

The Need for Religious Institutions

As the immigrants began to raise families, they felt a much greater need for religious institutions. Religion is the medium for passing on cultural values to children, and many of the Indians were concerned that their children would pick up bad habits in Western societies or even be drawn to convert to Christianity.

Bet You Didn't Know

In India, the grandparents are the main vehicle for religious education. They take the young ones to the local shrines and temples and tell them stories about saints and deities. But the grandparent generation is missing in the immigrant household.

It is quite different to learn about a religion in a country where it is part of daily life and is practiced by everyone around, than in a country where only a handful of members reside. In Western countries, there are no Hindu national holidays, no wandering *sadhus* to share spiritual knowledge, no traveling storytellers who recount the great epics. So the parents had to figure out how to explain a tradition that most of them had never really consciously tried to define to children growing up in a different cultural milieu.

Temples became the focal points for preserving tradition. Yet even as communities started to raise money to establish temples, they began to make numerous adaptations to their new environments. The first temples were converted buildings, often churches. Later communities raised enough money to build temples with traditional architecture. Many of these temples are partial replicas of temples in India that sponsor them. But the diaspora temples are uniquely ecumenical.

In an effort to meet the needs of the diverse immigrant communities, the temples include images of numerous deities instead of just one major deity and his or her retinue. Thus it is quite common to find Shiva and Vishnu standing side by side surrounded by various goddesses and regional deities.

Bet You Didn't Know

Shri Venkateshwara Temple in southern California has two adjacent areas of worship. The main complex is dedicated to Vishnu and houses images of several of the god's incarnations, but Shiva, his wife Parvati, and Ganesha preside over a second complex just beyond the temple wall.

The images in diaspora temples are made by traditional artisans in India and installed by Brahmin priests in time-honored fashion. A few temples have even tried to accommodate both northern and southern Indian constituencies by having images made of white marble for the northerners and black stone for the southerners.

Religious Festivals and Camps

Living in a non-Hindu land has also brought changes in temple calendars. Festivals are often celebrated on weekends instead of their proper dates according to the Hindu lunar calendar. This makes it easier for people to attend, especially when they must travel a long distance to reach the temple. Most temples hold regular services on weekends since that is when the largest number of people visit.

Temples also organize camps and classes for children to instruct them about Hindu *dharma* and values, and to teach them Indian languages. Children say they find a sense of relief and belonging in their camp experiences because they are in a fully Hindu environment where they do not feel any need to explain what they are doing or what they believe.

Bet You Didn't Know

In a "secular" Western country, Christianity pervades the school calendar (Sundays off, Christmas and Easter holidays) and children of other faiths often feel out of step with their schoolmates.

The urge to preserve cultural traditions for the next generation has led to the establishment of classes in Indian music and dance. Many temples have auditoriums for performances and kitchens for preparing community feasts, so they serve as community centers as well as religious sites.

The process of explaining Hinduism is aided by a burgeoning industry in educational literature, much of it published under the auspices of the Vishva Hindu Parishad. This is a logical step for an organization that wants to improve Hindu dharma and prevent conversion to other religions, but it also means that "orthodox" Hinduism is being defined by a particular group. The VHP in India is essentially urban and middle class, so its definitions may not include popular religion. But since the immigrant audience is also middle class, the interpretations fit their needs.

The Diaspora Institutions

Many of the elements of religious life considered folk tradition are missing in the diaspora. In Western countries, the temple deities receive only vegetarian offerings. There are no village goddesses being placated or cooled with blood sacrifice, and traditions of possession and folk healing techniques, which were seen in Hindu communities settled by laborers in the first wave of migrations, are usually missing from second-wave communities. This reflects the different class origins of the immigrants.

The establishment of Hindu religious institutions in foreign lands has been accompanied by some new problems. One such problem has been a lack of communication between the Hindus and the mainstream society. There have been minor problems about noise during all-night celebrations and complaints about too many cars parked in residential neighborhoods near temples during festivals, and major problems when Christian townsfolk fear that an Indian community may be trying to build a new Rajneeshpuram in their midst.

Such problems are usually resolved through discussion. Hindus are learning to reach out and share information about their religion so their neighbors will not equate their traditions with New Age cults, and Westerners are learning that Hinduism is a diverse tradition and the few extreme images that have appeared in world media are not representative.

Another issue for diaspora institutions is temple support. It is much easier to get people to donate for a temple construction project than to convince them to make the regular contributions necessary for upkeep. In India, land revenues support temples, but in other countries they must rely on their members. And here the problem of communalism reappears. As the immigrant communities grow, they tend to subdivide along regional-cultural lines. The ecumenical attitude of the early, smaller group breaks down. The Gujaratis start to want their own temple with regional deities, where the devotional songs will be sung in Gujarati, and the Bengalis want their own place. This tendency to develop divisions appears all over the world.

Another problem comes form the generation gap between the parents and their children. The children grow up mediating between two cultures. Most of them have great pride in their Indian heritage, but they are also affected by the cultural milieu in which they spend most of their school time. Growing up in Western societies, they often become uncomfortable with some of the practices of traditional Hinduism, especially image worship. Going to temple on weekends and spending some time at summer camp are not the same as living in the land made sacred by the physical presence of deities playing out their myths. Most American-raised Indians prefer a Neo-Vedanta type of Hinduism, with an emphasis on an impersonal Brahman.

Bet You Didn't Know

In Toronto, Canada, there is tension between the Tamils from Tamil Nadu and the Tamils from Sri Lanka. The Sri Lankans are the more recent arrivals but they now outnumber the Hindus from Tamil Nadu, and they are changing the way things are done at the temple both groups attend. Such communalism is threatening to undermine support of religious centers as the immigrant communities build more temples than they have the means to support.

Slowly, however, land outside of India is being sacralized by Hinduism. Prayers in the United States may substitute the Mississippi and Missouri Rivers for the Ganges and Yamuna, thereby making the waters of North America sacred. Clay images of Ganesha and other deities have been carried in procession through European and American streets and immersed in local waterways. The larger temples of Europe and the United States, with their traditional architecture and consecrated images, are becoming pilgrimage sites. And a Shiva *lingam* manifested in Golden Gate Park, San Francisco.

The dome-shaped stone appeared at a crossroads of three footpaths in the park, where some Hindus noticed it. They knew the stone had not been there before and immediately recognized it as a *lingam*, a manifestation of the god Shiva. Word spread and people began to visit the park to make offerings of flowers and fruit. Folk from the Shakti Mandir (temple) in San Francisco soon began to observe a regular worship service in the park, and gradually the stone became covered with sandalwood paste and adorned with garlands of flowers. The *lingam* became a place of pilgrimage for Hindus in the Bay Area. As it turns out, the *lingam* was originally a bollard, or street barrier, that the city had abandoned in the park. Recognizing that it had religious significance, the city helped move the stone to a private location because religious sites are not allowed on city property.

The modern Hinduism that is shared by urban communities all around the world has its roots in the ideals set forth by the reformers who began to redefine their religion in the nineteenth century. They turned to the heritage of Vedic philosophy for religious principles that could be adapted to the modern world. Revived respect for the wisdom of the ancient scriptures helped establish Hinduism as a great world religion, equal to Christianity and Islam. This, in turn, contributed to the development of nationalism, in which Hinduism provided the common language to give the people of India a sense of shared identity as a nation. But even though this national identity has been established, South Asia remains an area of great cultural diversity, and there are numerous forces working to influence modern Hinduism. Next, we examine some of the most prevalent trends shaping the future of this endlessly variable tradition.

The Least You Need to Know

- Leaders of the movement for India's independence from British rule used Hindu practices and ideals to muster support from the populace. They stressed the otherness of the English as followers of a foreign faith and characterized government laws that affected long-established traditions as attacks on the Hindu religion.

- There have been two waves of Hindu emigration in the modern period. The first occurred during the nineteenth and early twentieth centuries. The second wave, which really gained momentum in the 1960s and continues today, is made up of middle-class, educated urbanites.

- In an effort to meet the needs of the diverse immigrant communities, temples included images of multiple deities instead of just one major deity and his or her retinue.

11

Toward the Future

In This Chapter

- New trends: urban lifestyles and female leadership
- Regional strength
- Hinduism as a world religion

It has often been said that Hinduism never really gets rid of anything, new ideas and practices are simply added on and old philosophies are reinterpreted. Hinduism is essentially a tradition being eternally reborn, and the karmic impressions of the past and present are the forces that shape the future. This process will undoubtedly continue.

Hinduism has more than 3,000 years of diverse traditions from which to draw ideas and strength. The religion will be adapted to meet the needs of the future. At present, some of the trends affecting the shape of Hinduism are urbanization, changes in the religious roles of women, modern technology, continuing regionalism, and globalization.

Urbanization, and Fast!

Although nearly three quarters of the population in
South Asia still live in villages, the urban areas are
growing rapidly. Within the cities traditional patterns
give way to new adaptations in life and religion.
There is considerable disparity in the economic
circumstances of the city dwellers since some are
poor laborers seeking work and others are part of
an expanding middle class of educated, skilled professionals, but in many ways the social changes are
shared by both groups.

Inherited occupations are replaced by new types of
employment. Wealth and social status are no longer
based on land ownership, crops, and livestock, but on
cash incomes. People in the city are less likely to live
in extended families and cannot rely as often on kinship networks. In the city, caste divisions generally
carry less weight, except in matters of matrimony.
And sectarian affiliations often shift since the deities
of the village temple may not be present in the city.

The growth of the urban middle class in India has led
to the spread of a "modern" Hinduism that has many
similarities with Swami Vivekananda's Neo-Vedanta.
Most advocates of this modern Hinduism combine
religion with social concerns. They oppose the ideas
of caste and gender differentiation in spiritual education, and feel that the Hindu spirit is in need of
renewal. They believe religions should focus on the
well-being of the community, not just meditation.
Consequently, they are involved in efforts to "uplift"
untouchables and construct Hindu mission hospitals.

On the Right Path _____

Gurus also have an interest in the spiritual lives of overseas communities. The needs of the emigrants, who are mostly middle class, are much the same as the needs of their fellows in India. Both groups of Hindus talk about individual growth and social concerns, and see religion as a code of conduct. Their major focus is on success in life.

Modern gurus have become quite popular with a wide variety of people in urban areas. These gurus are the living arbiters of tradition. They adapt the ancient teachings to the needs of modern life. Many of them espouse a type of Neo-Vedanta, emphasizing the wisdom of pre-Puranic scriptures and the mystical vision of the poet-saints. They maintain that the Hindu philosophies contained in the Upanishads are the essence of all religions, so their teachings transcend sectarianism.

They describe God as an impersonal Absolute, permeating everything. Consequently there can be no caste pollution. They emphasize the importance of personal religious practices that train the mind and body, like meditation, chanting God's name, and singing devotional songs. These teachings combine instruction for living a virtuous life in the world and achieving higher knowledge to free oneself from the bonds of rebirth. But the traditions are also less place-bound than village religion. The emphasis on personal practices does not require residence in a particular place or attendance at a specific temple. These teachings are well suited to the mobility of urban life.

Women and Hinduism

Given the patriarchal emphasis in Hinduism over the last millennium, a surprising number of the modern gurus are women. The greater visibility of women as religious leaders is one of the important changes in modern Hinduism. This change has its roots in several areas, most notably the nineteenth- and twentieth-century Hindu reform movements, nationalism, and the independence movement, all of which laid foundations for the appreciation of feminine spirituality and established opportunities for its expression.

The nineteenth- and twentieth-century reform movements advocated a return to the pure Hindu traditions of the past as described in the Vedas and the Upanishads. In these texts, women were educated in the Vedic lore just like men. Women like Gargi appear in the texts taking part in scholarly debates with the men and acquitting themselves admirably. The reformers used these references as a basis to advocate education for both men and women as a necessary basis for an ideal Hindu society.

Furthermore, since in the Vedas women could speak in public forums and spend equal numbers of years in school as men, there were grounds for rejecting social practices like *purdah* (the seclusion of women), child-marriage, *sati*, and permanent widowhood. Because of this activism, social organizations of women emerged within both the Arya Samaj and the Brahmo Samaj.

Female Imagery

The use of female imagery in the nationalist movement and modern sects has contributed to the popular acceptance of women as religious leaders. The Bengali literati, in particular, wrote of Mother India, Bharat Mata, who had to be saved from the infidels who defiled her. The image of India as a mother goddess spread and has continued to gain popularity, reminding Hindus of all sects that the Absolute can take female form as easily as male. The symbol of the divine mother gradually came to be viewed as actually embodied in women ascetics. Recognition of the feminine aspect of God has also been reinforced in the last century by religious leaders whose teachings include the Tantric idea of Shakti as the feminine power of God.

Bet You Didn't Know

Ramakrishna gave momentum to the recognition of the feminine aspect of God when he worshiped his wife as the embodiment of the divine feminine. Since then, the idea of Shakti has become a common legitimation of the power of the female guru.

Finally, there was widespread involvement of women in the struggle for independence. Gandhi held up women as ideal moral models because they personified self-denial and inner strength. Gandhi's independence movement inspired a strong response among middle- and upper-class women who were transformed by their experience in the fight for freedom as they learned of their own abilities. The movement gave them an outlet for their energies and skills. They worked to organize people and spread information, they marched, and they went to jail. Their contributions were recognized within the movement where they attained high offices and influence.

Since independence, many women have continued to work for the betterment of society, following the ideals of *sarvodaya*, the uplift of all. But the advances experienced by women of the educated classes are not much evident in rural areas.

Equality?

Literacy rates for women are much lower than for men because boys receive more schooling than girls. The laws of India attempt to give women equal rights, but there is a great difference between laws on the books and common practices. Uneducated village women usually do not know about their legal rights. According to the Indian constitution, males and females are supposed to inherit equally, yet rural property remains almost entirely in male hands.

In many states, village councils have a seat reserved for a female member, but the local women are seldom aware of this provision, and even if they wanted to seek election and hold office, they would be faced with the daunting prospect of challenging long-established traditions. As the dichotomy between law and reality has been publicized, efforts are being made to reach out to village women. Programs organized and run mostly by women work to educate and make available resources to help others.

The inheritors of the reform movements have brought women new opportunities for religious life. Sarada Math is a women's monastic community that grew out of Vivekananda's Ramakrishna mission. Vivekananda had hoped to establish a women's group but had deemed the time not yet right. His vision became reality in 1954. Sarada offers women a chance to live in a monastic community run solely by women where they combine spiritual practices with social outreach through their schools and hospitals. Modern recognition of women's spiritual life is not limited to the greater opportunity for monastic life.

Women are also being recognized as gurus. A number of male gurus have named women as their successors, passing the responsibility for carrying on their teachings to female disciples. A few women have even become gurus on their own. Jnanananda Ma has been recognized by the Shankaracharya of Kanchipuram, one of the most respected arbiters of Hindu orthodoxy. She was already a well-established spiritual teacher in her householder days before she went to him to take vows of renunciation.

Another remarkable new opportunity for women has emerged in Maharashtra where women have been formally trained to carry out the duties of temple priests. The idea of priestesses is acceptable to many among the educated classes, who often say they think the women are more honest and pious than the men.

Bet You Didn't Know

Orthodox male priests have objected to women being formally trained as temple priests, on the grounds that to allow women to perform the rituals is a violation of Vedic law, but supporters point out that there is no actual prohibition against priestesses in the Vedas. The women are aided in their new employment by the increasing shortage of male priests. This is especially apparent in Hindu communities outside of South Asia where traditional specialists are in short supply and women often find themselves taking up new roles.

Strength of Regionalism

Regionalism is certainly one of the factors that will continue to affect Hinduism in the future. Local movements have always been the dynamic center for Hindu traditions. Individual identity is most closely tied to family and community allegiances even in this age of nationalism. Great power can be found in a unified group with shared concerns. People can turn to the local community as a source of strength for confronting problems affecting traditional village life as well as life in the urban diaspora. The Chipko movement is an example of a region unifying to confront problems affecting the village while the Swaminarayan tradition illustrates the strength of regional identity far from its homeland.

The Chipko Movement: Grass-roots Strength

In the Chipko movement, regional communities have united to challenge big business and government practices that create local problems. Chipko, the "tree-hugging" movement, grew out of the problems created by deforestation of the Himalayas. The trees were being cut down for industries in the plains. The hill villages received no economic benefit from the forestry but they lost their local sources of firewood and fodder. Furthermore, loss of vegetation caused loss of topsoil, ruining local agriculture so men had to migrate to the plains seeking work. The women who were left at home found their workloads increasing both from the extra labor of running homes without husbands and the extra distances they had to travel to collect wood. The deforestation also reduced rainwater retention in the hills, causing floods in the plains followed by droughts.

This escalating environmental disaster, carried forward by economic profits and industrialization's demand for wood, gave rise to the Chipko movement. The early impetus for Chipko came from Gandhian *sarvodaya* (uplift of all) workers who noted the problems the deforestation was creating for the villagers. They began to spread information about the value of trees and inspired local people to nonviolently protest the felling. The methods used to build the movement drew on Hindu religious traditions.

The primary means of communication was a footmarch, modeled on the religious pilgrimage, which took Chipko speakers to remote villages where they could share information. Folk songs proved an effective medium for spreading messages about the value of trees. This message had immediate resonance because reverence for trees has a long history in Hinduism, harking all the way back to the *Rig Veda*.

The modern Chipko workers have used their bodies to protect the trees, and their dedication has brought an end to indiscriminate cutting. Felling is no longer allowed in watershed areas and reforestation projects include locally necessary firewood and fodder trees as well as pine and fruit trees that produce cash crops. The government has realized that immediate profits do not justify long-term problems such as the destruction of village livelihoods and loss of watersheds, which leads to flood and drought cycles. The success of this movement is an inspiration to other areas of South Asia where government development is at odds with local needs and to communities with similar problems around the world.

On the Right Path

Chipko organized educational camps that were much like spiritual retreats. But one of the best ways to reach a wide audience was through stories of folk heroes. One of the most famous inspirational stories concerned Amrita Devi, a woman of the Bishnoi tribe in Rajasthan. Since the fifteenth century, this tribe has prohibited tree felling to preserve their local ecology. When a king sent axemen to cut trees for a new palace, Amrita Devi tried to protect a tree by hugging it. She was cut down, as were 362 other villagers who followed her example. The king heard about the massacre and pledged never again to cut Bishnoi trees.

Swaminarayan: A Regional Tradition Becomes International

The strength of religion as part of regional, cultural identity can be seen in the Swaminarayan tradition. Swaminarayan is a Gujarati form of Vaishnava Hinduism. It uses Hindu texts, focuses on devotion to the pan-Hindu god Vishnu, and practices Hindu rituals that would be recognized as part of Hinduism throughout South Asia. Yet the whole tradition is tied up in a specifically Gujarati ethnicity because the language, dress, cuisine, architecture, iconography, music, and dance are all drawn from the regional culture of Gujarat. Furthermore the religious leaders and sacred sites are in Gujarat.

This regional-ethnic Hinduism was begun in the nineteenth century by Sahajanand Swami (1781–1830), a follower of Ramanuja's qualified nondualism. The founder became known as Swaminarayan and was considered the *avatara* of Vishnu for the modern age. His teachings advocated a combination of devotion and worship with moral conduct (*dharma*) determined by age, gender, and social position. Followers are supposed to take part in devotional singing, serve the temple images, listen to religious discourses, and practice the mental worship of constantly remembering God.

This tradition is widespread in Gujarat, but it is even more prominent among Gujarati emigrants living in East Africa, England, and the United States. In the diaspora, Gujaratis join Swaminarayan to preserve their ethnic culture while taking in part in Hindu religious life. They build temples and organize cultural classes to pass on traditions to children. The temple ritual language, festival dress, foods, and entertainment are all Gujarati, so the tradition is quite distinct from the rest of the immigrant community.

This ethnically Gujarati Hinduism has become an international tradition. Festivals are now held in East Africa, England, and the United States. People come from all over the world to attend these events that offer an opportunity for global, social, and business contacts as well as religious observance. Modern technology makes it possible for this international

tradition to maintain close ties to its ethnic homeland. Air travel brings pilgrims to visit sacred sites
in Gujarat. These pilgrims then return to their new
countries carrying Gujarati publications, audiocas-
settes of Gujarati, devotional songs, and video tapes
of religious lectures by Gujarati *sadhus*.

World Religion

Hinduism, like Judaism, has become a world religion by means of migration, not missionization.
The religious tradition is closely tied to ethnic
cultures of South Asia. In spite of this, the urban,
middle-class Hinduism, or Neo-Vedanta, being
adopted by the international community as more
appropriate to their changed lifestyles also appeals
to Westerners. They particularly like the emphasis
on belief in an impersonal Absolute, tolerance of all
religions, and the perfectability of the individual.

Because most Westerners interested in Hinduism
only read texts, they tend to accept the philosophies without adopting the popular culture.
Practices of yoga and meditation have proven particularly suitable in the present era of "privatiza-
tion" of religion. These practices can be taken up
by the individual for private use on a path toward
personal spiritual attainment. The wisdom of the
East is being utilized as an alternative to the "fossilized doctrine" of the West. But this approach
leaves out the richness of popular tradition and
practice.

Hindu Hints

Westerners who take up yoga can completely divorce it from all religious context, viewing it as a mental and physical exercise designed to calm the mind and strengthen the body. Most of these yogic practitioners have never been into a Hindu temple, have never seen the art and architecture that makes the sacred manifest on earth, have never made offerings of thanks for a child's recovery from illness, have never chanted the name of God hoping for a vision of the Deity, and do not mark their calendars by the festivals in honor of Krishna's birthday and Rama's triumph over the demon Ravana.

Halfway between the Westerners who like Hindu philosophy and the immigrant traditionalists are the children who have grown up in the diaspora. This second generation has had to balance its South Asian cultural heritage with ideals adopted from Western society. For this second generation, Hinduism is as much a part of their cultural identity as part of a genuine spirituality. In their personal beliefs, they tend to prefer Neo-Vedanta because the same attributes that make it appealing to people outside the traditional Hindu cultural sphere also work for Indian-Americans and Indian-Europeans.

Children who grow up in Western countries are also having their own effect on traditions. Despite the educational efforts of their parents, members of the second generation are rarely fluent in Indian languages. They may speak and understand them, but they cannot read well enough to tackle the great religious literatures. Consequently, English is becoming more prominent in texts and rituals. The loss of languages with regional-cultural ties may be a factor in the changed sense of identity in the second generation.

Where the parents think of themselves as Gujaratis and Tamils, the children consider themselves "Indians" and have little patience for the regional and caste differentiations made by their parents. Some young folks have expressed a hope that their generation, with its shared experiences of growing up between two cultures, will be able to transcend these prejudices. The unified identity of the second generation will lead to new adaptations in Hinduism, especially if these young people begin to feel a greater interest in religion as they start to raise families of their own.

Hinduism Worldview

Over the last two centuries, Hinduism has become a world religion. In the process, Hindus have been working to define their traditions externally, in relation to other religions, and internally, where social and regional divisions create such tremendous diversity. Scholars who focus on the richness of this diversity argue that one should not speak of "Hinduism" but rather of "Hinduisms." Yet in spite of these variations in tradition, modern Hindus recognize themselves as belonging to one religious community. This growing communal identity, extending far beyond local and sectarian allegiances, will be a major factor in shaping the future of the religion.

The process of religious adaptation and redefinition that has gone on for thousands of years is by no means at an end. The modern Hindu community will continue this process, influenced by tensions between tradition and innovation, rural and urban needs, diversity and unification.

By drawing on the richness of the past and the strength of proven systems and then using these to filter new ideas and shape modifications, Hinduism is adapting to the needs of an extended global community. Local traditions offer foundations for structuring local innovations more appropriate than any changes imposed from outside. And modern technology brings communication and connections to build an extended community even while making available new information and ideas that inspire local changes.

As circumstances shift, philosophies are adapted, rituals are revised and reinterpreted, and the Divine is reimagined. Through it all Hinduism, like the individual Self, takes on new embodiments time after time in a continuing cycle. It is a tradition being eternally reborn.

The Least You Need to Know

- The growth of the urban middle class in India has led to the spread of a "modern" Hinduism that combines religion with social concerns.

- The use of female imagery in the nationalist movement and modern sects has contributed to the popular acceptance of women as religious leaders.

- The Chipko movement is an example of a region unifying to confront problems affecting the village while the Swaminarayan tradition illustrates the strength of regional identity far from its homeland.

- Swaminarayan is a Gujarati form of Vaishnava Hinduism. It uses Hindu texts, focuses on devotion to the pan-Hindu god Vishnu, and practices Hindu rituals that are recognized as part of Hinduism throughout South Asia.

- Hindus have been working to define their traditions externally, in relation to other religions, and internally, where social and regional divisions create such tremendous diversity.

Glossary

Advaita   Non-duality, name of a school of Vedanta.

ahimsa   Non-injury.

Aranyaka   Forest book, texts explaining the Vedic rituals.

arati   Waving a flame or lamp during worship.

ashrama   Stage of life.

atman   The individual self.

avatara   Incarnation of a god.

bhakti   Love, devotion.

bhakti-yoga   The path of devotion.

bindu   The point at the center of a *mandala*.

Brahma   The creator god.

brahman   Divine power, the power of the Vedic *mantras*.

Brahman   The Absolute.

Brahmana   Text explaining the performance and meaning of the Vedic rituals.

brahmin   The priestly caste (*varna*).

camiyati   God dancer in south India.

chakra   "Circle"; centers along the subtle spinal channel in Tantra.

communalism   Defining of group by religious identity.

darshan   Vision, being in the presence of divinity.

deva   Deity.

Devi   The great goddess.

dharma   Law, virtue, duty, correct behavior, religion.

garbha-griha   Womb-house; the inner sanctuary of a temple.

Gayatri   A Vedic *mantra*.

gopi   Milkmaid, the devotees of Krishna.

gopuram   Gate-tower for a south Indian temple.

gunas   Inherent qualities of the universe.

guru   Spiritual teacher.

Hindutva   Hinduness.

ishtadevata   One's chosen god.

jati   Birth group, caste.

jnana-yoga   The path of knowledge.

Kali Yuga   Dark age.

karma-yoga   The path of action.

karman   Action, the acts that affect one's experiences after death and in the next life.

kirtan   Devotional singing.

kshatriya   The warrior caste (*varna*).

lila   Play, especially divine play.

lingam   The nonrepresentational image of Shiva.

lokasangraha   For the sake of the world.

mantra   Sacred word or formula.

math   Monastery.

maya   Divine illusion.

moksha   Liberation from the cycle of rebirth.

murti   Embodiment of the divine, image.

nirguna Brahman   Brahman without attributes.

prakriti   Materiality, the feminine matter from which the cosmos is formed.

prasada   Grace of God; ritual offerings given to devotees.

puja   Worship.

Purana   Old books.

Purusha   The divine person.

purusha   Consciousness that partners *prakriti* in creation.

rishi Seer.

rita Cosmic order.

sadhu Holy man, renunciant.

saguna Brahman Brahman with attributes.

samhita Collection, the Vedic collections of hymns, songs, chants, and spells.

samsara The cycle of rebirth.

samskara Life-cycle ritual.

sannyasa Renunciation.

sarvodaya Uplift of all.

Sati Wife of Shiva; term for widow suicide.

satsang Keeping the company of bhaktas (devotees of God).

Shaiva A devotee of the god Shiva.

Shakta A devotee of the goddess Devi.

Shakti The feminine divine power.

shalagrama Nonrepresentational image of Vishnu.

sharaddha Rites for the dead.

shikara Conical dome over a northern temple.

Shiva Supreme deity for many Hindus: god of *yoga*; known as god of creation and destruction.

shruti "That which is heard"; revelation.

shudra The peasant caste (*varna*).

smriti   "That which is remembered"; tradition.

Tantra   System of practices.

upanayana   Initiation, sacred-thread ceremony.

Upanishads   Texts, last addition to the Vedas.

Vaishnava   A devotee of the god Vishnu.

vaishya   The merchant/artisan/farming caste (*varna*).

varna   The four castes.

varnashrama-dharma   Duty according to caste and stage of life.

Veda   Knowledge; the early scriptures.

Vishishta-advaita   Qualified nonduality name of a school of Vedanta.

Vishnu   Supreme deity for many Hindus: associated with 10 incarnations, known as Preserver.

vrata   Votive observance.

yantra   Diagram used to aid meditation. The patterns represent the cosmos and the process of creation.

yoga   Discipline.

yogin   One who practices yoga.

yoni   Nonrepresentational image of Devi.

yuga   Aeon, age.

Index